# Contents

Introduction .... **5**

January: 31 Days | Strength .... **10**

February: 29 Days | Faith .... **42**

March: 31 Days | Seeking Purpose .... **72**

April: 30 Days | Love .... **104**

May: 31 Days | Learning to Trust God .... **135**

June: 30 Days | Use What's in Your Hands..**167**

July: 31 Days | Overcoming Rejection .... **198**

August: 31 Days | Overcoming Fear .... **230**

September: 30 Days | The Voice of God . **262**

October: 31 Days | Healing .... **293**

November: 30 Days | Forgiveness .... **325**

December: 31 Days | New Beginnings .... **356**

Afterword .... **389**

Scriptural References | Holy Bible .... **393**

*365 Days Affirmed*

*Amen Somebody!*

*365 Days Affirmed*

*Amen Somebody!*

# Introduction:

In the tapestry of our lives, woven with the threads of joy and challenges, there exists a profound truth – the power of affirmations to shape our reality. Welcome to *365 Days Affirmed* a transformative journey into the realm of self-discovery and empowerment.

In a world that often pulls us in myriad directions, leaving us searching for a sanctuary within ourselves, affirmations serve as beacons of light. They are the whispers of encouragement that echo within, reminding us of our innate strength, resilience, and the limitless possibilities that reside in the core of our being.

This book is a curated collection of affirmations, carefully crafted to inspire, uplift, and guide you on your path to self-realization. Each page invites you to pause, breathe, and reflect on the beauty that exists within you. Affirmations, like seeds planted in the fertile soil of your mind, have the power to sprout into a garden of positivity, fostering a mindset of abundance and self-love.

This journal ends each day's personal affirmation with the phrase "Amen Somebody." "Amen" is a term of significant importance in the Bible, conveying affirmation, agreement, and truthfulness. Its roots are in Hebrew, where it means "certainty" or "truth." In a Biblical context, "Amen" is often used to affirm the trustworthiness and reliability of God's Words and promises. This is a phrase that transcends mere words. It is a sacred mantra, embodying the finality of "it is done" — a powerful affirmation of faith and acceptance.

Each time these words are spoken, they are not merely agreeing with the present; they are

*Amen Somebody!*

reverencing the divine choreography of life itself, acknowledging that every moment, every challenge, and every joy is part of a greater plan.

To say "Amen Somebody" is to recognize the presence of God in everything — from the golden rays of the morning sun to the trials that test the human spirit. Faith is not just a Sunday ritual; it is woven into the fabric of our existence. Speaking it in all interactions, whether with a friend or a stranger, there's an unspoken invitation to join in this acknowledgment of a higher power. It inspires those around to look beyond the immediate, to see the Divine Hand in the mundane. It is a continuous act of worship, where "Amen Somebody" serves as a constant reminder that in every situation, God is present, and His will prevails.

As an author, my intention is not just to offer you words on paper but to provide you with a companion for your journey. *365 Days Affirmed* is a mirror reflecting the brilliance that already exists within you, waiting to be acknowledged and celebrated. Through the art of positive affirmations, we embark on a quest to unveil the potential that resides in the depths of your soul.

Whether you are seeking solace in times of uncertainty, striving for personal growth, or simply yearning for a daily dose of inspiration, this book is a sanctuary for your spirit. The affirmations within these pages are crafted with intention, designed to resonate with the rhythm of your heart and awaken the dormant possibilities that lie dormant within.

So, dear reader, open the pages of *365 Days Affirmed* with an open heart and a curious mind. Let the affirmations within be your guiding stars, lighting the path to a more profound connection with yourself. May this collection serve as a

*Amen Somebody!*

gentle reminder that within you, there is a reservoir of strength, love, and resilience waiting to be discovered and embraced, through Christ.

Here's to the journey of self-discovery, empowerment, and the radiant reflections that illuminate our path.

With warmth and encouragement,

Theresa Y. Brown, *Mrs. Amen Somebody* ...

# January: 31 Days | Strength

*Amen Somebody!*

## Day 1: Inner Strength

**Affirmation**: I am strong and resilient, capable of overcoming any challenge.

*Philippians 4:13 - "I can do all things through Christ who strengthens me."*

**Reflective Question**: What challenges have I overcome that demonstrate my inner strength?

_____
_____
_____
_____

**My Personal Affirmation for Today:**

_____
_____
_____
_____

*Amen Somebody!*

## Day 2: Courage

**Affirmation**: I am courageous and face my fears with confidence.

*Joshua 1:9 - "Be strong and courageous. Do not be afraid; do not be discouraged, for the Lord your God will be with you wherever you go."*

**Reflective Question**: How can I show courage in my daily life?

_____
_____
_____
_____

**My Personal Affirmation for Today:**

_____
_____
_____
_____

*Amen Somebody!*

## Day 3: Perseverance

**Affirmation**: I persevere through difficulties, knowing each step makes me stronger.

*James 1:12 - "Blessed is the one who perseveres under trial because, having stood the test, that person will receive the crown of life that the Lord has promised to those who love Him."*

**Reflective Question**: In what areas of my life do I need to show more perseverance?

_____

_____

_____

_____

**My Personal Affirmation for Today:**

_____

_____

_____

_____

***Amen Somebody!***

## Day 4: Confidence

**Affirmation**: I am confident in my abilities and trust in my inner wisdom.

*Proverbs 3:26 - "For the Lord will be your confidence and will keep your foot from being caught."*

**Reflective Question**: How does my confidence shape the decisions I make?

_____
_____
_____
_____

**My Personal Affirmation for Today:**

_____
_____
_____
_____

*Amen Somebody!*

## Day 5: Overcoming Fear

**Affirmation**: I overcome my fears with faith and determination.

*Isaiah 41:10 - "So do not fear, for I am with you; do not be dismayed, for I am your God. I will strengthen you and help you; I will uphold you with my righteous right hand."*

**Reflective Question**: What fears have I conquered recently, and how did I do it?

_____

_____

_____

_____

**My Personal Affirmation for Today:**

_____

_____

_____

_____

*Amen Somebody!*

*365 Days Affirmed*

## Day 6: Self-Belief

**Affirmation**: I believe in myself and my ability to succeed.

*Mark 9:23 - "Everything is possible for one who believes."*

**Reflective Question**: How does my belief in myself influence my actions and goals?

_____
_____
_____
_____

**My Personal Affirmation for Today:**

_____
_____
_____
_____

****Amen Somebody!***

## Day 7: Resilience

**Affirmation**: I am resilient and bounce back from setbacks.

*Psalm 46:1-2 - "God is our refuge and strength, an ever-present help in trouble. Therefore we will not fear, though the earth give way and the mountains fall into the heart of the sea."*

**Reflective Question**: How have I demonstrated resilience in difficult times?

_____

_____

_____

_____

**My Personal Affirmation for Today:**

_____

_____

_____

_____

*Amen Somebody!*

## Day 8: Inner Peace

**Affirmation**: I am at peace with myself and accept my strengths and weaknesses.

*John 14:27 - "Peace I leave with you; my peace I give you. I do not give to you as the world gives. Do not let your hearts be troubled and do not be afraid."*

**Reflective Question**: What steps can I take to cultivate more inner peace?

_____

_____

_____

_____

**My Personal Affirmation for Today:**

_____

_____

_____

_____

**_Amen Somebody!_**

*Amen Somebody!*

## Day 9: Hope

**Affirmation**: I am hopeful and optimistic about the future.

*Romans 15:13 - "May the God of hope fill you with all joy and peace as you trust in Him, so that you may overflow with hope by the power of the Holy Spirit."*

**Reflective Question**: What am I most hopeful for in my life right now?

_____
_____
_____
_____

**My Personal Affirmation for Today:**

_____
_____
_____
_____

*Amen Somebody!*

## Day 10: Gratitude

**Affirmation**: I am grateful for my strengths and the opportunities they bring."

*1 Thessalonians 5:18 - "Give thanks in all circumstances; for this is God's will for you in Christ Jesus."*

**Reflective Question**: What strengths am I most thankful for, and how have they benefited me?

_____
_____
_____
_____

**My Personal Affirmation for Today:**

_____
_____
_____
_____

***Amen Somebody!***

## Day 11: Empowerment

**Affirmation**: I am empowered to make positive changes in my life.

*2 Timothy 1:7 - "For God has not given us a spirit of fear, but of power and of love and of a sound mind."*

**Reflective Question**: What positive changes have I made recently, and how have they impacted me?

_____

_____

_____

_____

**My Personal Affirmation for Today:**

_____

_____

_____

*Amen Somebody!*

## Day 12: Wisdom

**Affirmation**: I seek and apply wisdom in all aspects of my life.

*James 1:5 - "If any of you lacks wisdom, you should ask God, who gives generously to all without finding fault, and it will be given to you."*

**Reflective Question**: How has wisdom played a role in my recent decisions?

_____

_____

_____

_____

**My Personal Affirmation for Today:**

_____

_____

_____

_____

***Amen Somebody!***

*Amen Somebody!*

## Day 13: Growth

**Affirmation**: I am committed to personal growth and learning.

*Ephesians 4:15 - "Instead, speaking the truth in love, we will grow to become in every respect the mature body of him who is the head, that is, Christ."*

**Reflective Question**: In what areas am I currently growing, and what am I learning?

_____
_____
_____
_____

**My Personal Affirmation for Today:**

_____
_____
_____
_____

*Amen Somebody!*

## Day 14: Love

**Affirmation**: I am filled with love for myself and others.

*1 Corinthians 16:14 - "Do everything in love."*

**Reflective Question**: How do I show love to myself and those around me?

_____

_____

_____

_____

**My Personal Affirmation for Today:**

_____

_____

_____

_____

*Amen Somebody!*

## Day 15: Purpose

**Affirmation**: I am driven by a strong sense of purpose and direction.

*Jeremiah 29:11 - "For I know the plans I have for you," declares the Lord, "plans to prosper you and not to harm you, plans to give you hope and a future."*

**Reflective Question**: What do I feel is my purpose, and how am I pursuing it?

_____

_____

_____

_____

**My Personal Affirmation for Today:**

_____

_____

_____

_____

*Amen Somebody!*

## Day 16: Joy

**Affirmation**: I find joy in my strengths and celebrate my achievements.

*Nehemiah 8:10 - "The joy of the Lord is your strength."*

**Reflective Question**: What recent achievements have brought me joy?

_____

_____

_____

_____

**My Personal Affirmation for Today:**

_____

_____

_____

_____

***Amen Somebody!***

## Day 17: Balance

**Affirmation**: I maintain a healthy balance between strength and gentleness.

*Matthew 5:5 - "Blessed are the meek, for they will inherit the earth."*

**Reflective Question**: How do I find balance in my life?

_____

_____

_____

_____

**My Personal Affirmation for Today:**

_____

_____

_____

*Amen Somebody!*

## Day 18: Harmony

**Affirmation**: I live in harmony with myself and my surroundings.

*Romans 12:18 - "If it is possible, as far as it depends on you, live at peace with everyone."*

**Reflective Question**: What steps can I take to create more harmony in my life?

_____

_____

_____

**My Personal Affirmation for Today:**

_____

_____

_____

*Amen Somebody!*

## Day 19: Authenticity

**Affirmation**: I am authentic and true to myself.

*1 Samuel 16:7 - "The Lord does not look at the things people look at. People look at the outward appearance, but the Lord looks at the heart."*

**Reflective Question**: How do I stay true to myself in various situations?

_____

_____

_____

_____

**My Personal Affirmation for Today:**

_____

_____

_____

_____

*Amen Somebody!*

*365 Days Affirmed*

**Day 20: Compassion**

**Affirmation**: I show compassion to myself and others.

*Colossians 3:12 - "Therefore, as God's chosen people, holy and dearly loved, clothe yourselves with compassion, kindness, humility, gentleness and patience."*

**Reflective Question**: How have I demonstrated compassion recently?

_____
_____
_____
_____

**My Personal Affirmation for Today:**

_____
_____
_____
_____

*Amen Somebody!*

## Day 21: Determination

**Affirmation**: I am determined and focused on my goals.

*1 Corinthians 9:24 - "Do you not know that in a race all the runners run, but only one gets the prize? Run in such a way as to get the prize."*

**Reflective Question**: What goals am I currently focused on?

_____

_____

_____

_____

**My Personal Affirmation for Today:**

_____

_____

_____

*Amen Somebody!*

## Day 22: Inspiration

**Affirmation**: I inspire and uplift those around me.

*Hebrews 10:24 - "And let us consider how we may spur one another on toward love and good deeds."*

**Reflective Question**: How do I inspire others in my daily life?

_____

_____

_____

_____

**My Personal Affirmation for Today:**

_____

_____

_____

_____

*Amen Somebody!*

## Day 23: Mindfulness

**Affirmation**: I am mindful and present in every moment.

*Psalm 46:10 - "Be still and know that I am God; I will be exalted among the nations, I will be exalted in the earth."*

**Reflective Question**: How do I practice mindfulness in my daily routine?

_____

_____

_____

_____

**My Personal Affirmation for Today:**

_____

_____

_____

_____

*Amen Somebody!*

## Day 24: Generosity

**Affirmation**: I am generous with my strengths, sharing them with others.

*Proverbs 11:25 - "A generous person will prosper; whoever refreshes others will be refreshed."*

**Reflective Question**: In what ways have I been generous recently?

_____

_____

_____

**My Personal Affirmation for Today:**

_____

_____

_____

*Amen Somebody!*

## Day 25: Patience

**Affirmation**: I am patient with myself and my progress.

*Galatians 6:9 - "Let us not become weary in doing good, for at the proper time we will reap a harvest if we do not give up."*

**Reflective Question**: How do I practice patience in my personal growth?

_____
_____
_____
_____

**My Personal Affirmation for Today:**

_____
_____
_____
_____

*Amen Somebody!*

## Day 26: Integrity

**Affirmation**: I act with integrity and honor in all aspects of my life.

*Proverbs 10:9 - "Whoever walks in integrity walks securely, but whoever takes crooked paths will be found out."*

**Reflective Question**: How do I ensure I maintain integrity in my actions?

_____
_____
_____
_____

**My Personal Affirmation for Today:**

_____
_____
_____

***Amen Somebody!***

**Day 27: Creativity**

**Affirmation**: I embrace my creativity and use it as a source of strength.

*Exodus 35:31-32 - "And he has filled him with the Spirit of God, with wisdom, with understanding, with knowledge and with all kinds of skills—to make artistic designs for work in gold, silver and bronze."*

**Reflective Question**: How does my creativity enhance my life and the lives of others?

_____
_____
_____
_____

**My Personal Affirmation for Today:**

_____
_____
_____
_____

*Amen Somebody!*

## Day 28: Humility

**Affirmation**: I remain humble and learn from every experience.

*James 4:6 - "But he gives us more grace. That is why Scripture says: 'God opposes the proud but shows favor to the humble."*

**Reflective Question**: How has humility played a role in my recent experiences?

_____
_____
_____
_____

**My Personal Affirmation for Today:**

_____
_____
_____

***Amen Somebody!***

## Day 29: Forgiveness

**Affirmation**: I practice forgiveness, releasing myself and others from past burdens.

*Ephesians 4:32 - "Be kind and compassionate to one another, forgiving each other, just as in Christ God forgave you."*

**Reflective Question**: How has forgiveness improved my life and relationships?

_____
_____
_____
_____

**My Personal Affirmation for Today:**

_____
_____
_____
_____

*Amen Somebody!*

## Day 30: Celebration

**Affirmation**: I celebrate my strengths and victories, big and small.

*Psalm 150:6 - "Let everything that has breath praise the Lord. Praise the Lord."*

**Reflective Question**: What recent victories or strengths can I celebrate today?

_____
_____
_____
_____

**My Personal Affirmation for Today:**

_____
_____
_____
_____

***Amen Somebody!***

## Day 31: Endurance

**Affirmation**: Even when things don't go as planned, I will continue to do good and make the right choices for my life.

*Galatians 6:9 - "Let us not grow weary in doing what is right, for if we do not give up, we will reap our harvest in due time."*

**Reflective Question**: What recent victories or strengths can I celebrate today?

_____

_____

_____

_____

**My Personal Affirmation for Today:**

_____

_____

_____

_____

*Amen Somebody!*

# February: 29 Days | Faith

*Amen Somebody!*

## Day 1: Trust in Faith

**Affirmation**: I trust in my faith to guide me through life's challenges.

*Proverbs 3:5-6 - "Trust in the Lord with all your heart and lean not on your own understanding; in all your ways submit to him, and he will make your paths straight."*

**Reflective Question**: How has my faith guided me in difficult times?

_____

_____

_____

_____

**My Personal Affirmation for Today:**

_____

_____

_____

_____

*Amen Somebody!*

## Day 2: Strength in Belief

**Affirmation**: My belief is a source of strength in my life.

*Isaiah 40:31 - "But those who hope in the Lord will renew their strength. They will soar on wings like eagles; they will run and not grow weary, they will walk and not be faint."*

**Reflective Question**: In what ways has my belief given me strength?

_____

_____

_____

_____

**My Personal Affirmation for Today:**

_____

_____

_____

_____

*Amen Somebody!*

## Day 3: Divine Guidance

**Affirmation**: I am guided by a divine power greater than myself.

*Psalm 32:8 - "I will instruct you and teach you in the way you should go; I will counsel you with my loving eye on you."*

**Reflective Question**: When have I felt most guided by my faith?

_____

_____

_____

_____

**My Personal Affirmation for Today:**

_____

_____

_____

*Amen Somebody!*

*365 Days Affirmed*

## Day 4: Unwavering Faith

**Affirmation**: My faith is unwavering, even in times of uncertainty.

*Hebrews 11:1 - "Now faith is confidence in what we hope for and assurance about what we do not see."*

**Reflective Question**: How do I maintain my faith during uncertain times?

_____

_____

_____

_____

**My Personal Affirmation for Today:**

_____

_____

_____

_____

*Amen Somebody!*

## Day 5: Peace Through Faith

**Affirmation**: I find peace through my faith.

*John 14:27 - "Peace I leave with you; my peace I give you. I do not give to you as the world gives. Do not let your hearts be troubled and do not be afraid."*

**Reflective Question**: How does my faith bring peace into my life?

_____

_____

_____

_____

**My Personal Affirmation for Today:**

_____

_____

_____

*Amen Somebody!*

## Day 6: Faith in Action

**Affirmation**: I put my faith into action every day.

*James 2:17 - "In the same way, faith by itself, if it is not accompanied by action, is dead."*

**Reflective Question**: What actions have I taken recently that demonstrate my faith?

_____
_____
_____
_____

**My Personal Affirmation for Today:**

_____
_____
_____
_____

*Amen Somebody!*

## Day 7: Gratitude in Faith

**Affirmation**: I am grateful for the blessings my faith brings into my life.

*1 Thessalonians 5:18 - "Give thanks in all circumstances; for this is God's will for you in Christ Jesus."*

**Reflective Question**: What aspects of my life am I most grateful for due to my faith?

_____
_____
_____
_____

**My Personal Affirmation for Today:**

_____
_____
_____
_____

*Amen Somebody!*

## Day 8: Hope and Faith

**Affirmation**: My faith fills me with hope for the future.

*Romans 15:13 - "May the God of hope fill you with all joy and peace as you trust in Him, so that you may overflow with hope by the power of the Holy Spirit."*

**Reflective Question**: How does my faith give me hope in challenging times?

_____

_____

_____

_____

**My Personal Affirmation for Today:**

_____

_____

_____

_____

***Amen Somebody!***

### Day 9: Love and Faith

**Affirmation**: My faith teaches me to love unconditionally.

*1 Corinthians 13:13 - "And now these three remain: faith, hope and love. But the greatest of these is love."*

**Reflective Question**: How does my faith influence the way I love others?

_____

_____

_____

_____

**My Personal Affirmation for Today:**

_____

_____

_____

_____

*Amen Somebody!*

## Day 10: Faith in Myself

**Affirmation**: I have faith in my abilities and potential.

*Philippians 4:13 - "I can do all things through Christ who strengthens me."*

**Reflective Question**: How does my faith empower my self-belief?

_____
_____
_____
_____

**My Personal Affirmation for Today:**

_____
_____
_____
_____

*Amen Somebody!*

## Day 11: Spiritual Growth

**Affirmation:** My faith is a journey of continual spiritual growth.

*2 Peter 3:18 - "But grow in the grace and knowledge of our Lord and Savior Jesus Christ. To him be glory both now and forever! Amen."*

**Reflective Question:** In what ways am I growing spiritually?

_____
_____
_____
_____

**My Personal Affirmation for Today:**

_____
_____
_____

*Amen Somebody!*

## Day 12: Faith and Forgiveness

**Affirmation**: Through my faith, I find the strength to forgive.

*Ephesians 4:32 - "Be kind and compassionate to one another, forgiving each other, just as in Christ God forgave you."*

**Reflective Question**: How has my faith helped me to forgive others?

_____

_____

_____

_____

**My Personal Affirmation for Today:**

_____

_____

_____

_____

*Amen Somebody!*

## Day 13: Resilience in Faith

**Affirmation**: My faith makes me resilient in the face of adversity.

*Romans 5:3-4 - "Not only so, but we also glory in our sufferings, because we know that suffering produces perseverance; perseverance, character; and character, hope."*

**Reflective Question**: How has my faith helped me to overcome challenges?

_____

_____

_____

_____

**My Personal Affirmation for Today:**

_____

_____

_____

_____

*Amen Somebody!*

## Day 14: Faith and Community

**Affirmation**: My faith connects me to a community of support and love.

*Hebrews 10:24-25 - "And let us consider how we may spur one another on toward love and good deeds, not giving up meeting together, as some are in the habit of doing, but encouraging one another—and all the more as you see the Day approaching."*

**Reflective Question**: How does my faith community support my spiritual journey?

_____

_____

_____

_____

**My Personal Affirmation for Today:**

_____

_____

_____

*Amen Somebody!*

*Amen Somebody!*

## Day 15: Faith in Difficult Times

**Affirmation**: In difficult times, my faith is my anchor.

*Psalm 46:1 - "God is our refuge and strength, an ever-present help in trouble."*

**Reflective Question**: How has my faith sustained me in difficult times?

_____

_____

_____

_____

**My Personal Affirmation for Today:**

_____

_____

_____

*Amen Somebody!*

## Day 16: Faith and Wisdom

**Affirmation**: My faith enriches me with wisdom. *James 1:5 - "If any of you lacks wisdom, you should ask God, who gives generously to all without finding fault, and it will be given to you."*

**Reflective Question**: How has faith contributed to my wisdom in life decisions?

_____

_____

_____

_____

**My Personal Affirmation for Today:**

_____

_____

_____

_____

*Amen Somebody!*

## Day 17: Faith and Patience

**Affirmation**: My faith teaches me patience and timing.

*Galatians 6:9 - "Let us not become weary in doing good, for at the proper time we will reap a harvest if we do not give up."*

**Reflective Question**: How has patience, guided by my faith, benefited me?

_____

_____

_____

_____

**My Personal Affirmation for Today:**

_____

_____

_____

*Amen Somebody!*

## Day 18: Faith and Healing

**Affirmation**: My faith brings healing to my mind, body, and spirit.

*Jeremiah 17:14 - "Heal me, Lord, and I will be healed; save me and I will be saved, for you are the one I praise."*

**Reflective Question**: In what ways has my faith contributed to my healing?

_____
_____
_____
_____

**My Personal Affirmation for Today:**

_____
_____
_____
_____

*Amen Somebody!*

## Day 19: Faith and Joy

**Affirmation**: My faith fills my life with joy and contentment.

*Psalm 28:7 - "The Lord is my strength and my shield; my heart trusts in him, and he helps me. My heart leaps for joy, and with my song I praise him."*

**Reflective Question**: How does my faith bring joy into my daily life?

_____

_____

_____

_____

**My Personal Affirmation for Today:**

_____

_____

_____

_____

*Amen Somebody!*

## Day 20: Faith and Purpose

**Affirmation**: My faith gives me a sense of purpose and direction.

*Proverbs 19:21 - "Many are the plans in a person's heart, but it is the Lord's purpose that prevails."*

**Reflective Question**: How does my faith influence my sense of purpose?

_____
_____
_____
_____

**My Personal Affirmation for Today:**
_____
_____
_____
_____

*Amen Somebody!*

## Day 21: Faith in the Future

**Affirmation**: I have faith that the future holds great things for me.

*Jeremiah 29:11 - "For I know the plans I have for you," declares the Lord, "plans to prosper you and not to harm you, plans to give you hope and a future."*

**Reflective Question**: What am I hopeful for in my future due to my faith?

_____
_____
_____
_____

**My Personal Affirmation for Today:**

_____
_____
_____
_____

*Amen Somebody!*

## Day 22: Faith and Generosity

**Affirmation**: My faith inspires me to be generous and kind.

*2 Corinthians 9:7 - "Each of you should give what you have decided in your heart to give, not reluctantly or under compulsion, for God loves a cheerful giver."*

**Reflective Question**: How does my faith motivate me to be generous?

_____
_____
_____
_____

**My Personal Affirmation for Today:**

_____
_____
_____
_____

***Amen Somebody!***

## Day 23: Faith and Humility

**Affirmation**: My faith teaches me humility and gratitude.

*James 4:6 - "But he gives us more grace. That is why Scripture says: 'God opposes the proud but shows favor to the humble.'"*

**Reflective Question**: How does my faith help me stay humble and grateful?

_____

_____

_____

_____

**My Personal Affirmation for Today:**

_____

_____

_____

_____

*Amen Somebody!*

## Day 24: Faith and Integrity

**Affirmation**: I live my life with integrity, guided by my faith.

*Proverbs 11:3 - "The integrity of the upright guides them, but the unfaithful are destroyed by their duplicity."*

**Reflective Question**: How does my faith influence my integrity?

_____
_____
_____
_____

**My Personal Affirmation for Today:**

_____
_____
_____
_____

*Amen Somebody!*

## Day 25: Faith and Compassion

**Affirmation**: My faith fills me with compassion for others.

*Colossians 3:12 - "Therefore, as God's chosen people, holy and dearly loved, clothe yourselves with compassion, kindness, humility, gentleness and patience."*

**Reflective Question**: How do I show compassion in a way that reflects my faith?

_____

_____

_____

_____

**My Personal Affirmation for Today:**

_____

_____

_____

*Amen Somebody!*

## Day 26: Faith and Endurance

**Affirmation**: My faith gives me the endurance to persevere.

*Hebrews 12:1 - "Therefore, since we are surrounded by such a great cloud of witnesses, let us throw off everything that hinders and the sin that so easily entangles. And let us run with perseverance the race marked out for us."*

**Reflective Question**: How has my faith helped me persevere through tough times?

_____
_____
_____
_____

**My Personal Affirmation for Today:**

_____
_____
_____
_____

*Amen Somebody!*

## Day 27: Faith and Mindfulness

**Affirmation**: I practice mindfulness, staying present and grounded in my faith.

*Psalm 46:10 - "Be still and know that I am God; I will be exalted among the nations, I will be exalted in the earth."*

**Reflective Question**: How does mindfulness enhance my faith experience?

_____

_____

_____

_____

**My Personal Affirmation for Today:**

_____

_____

_____

_____

*Amen Somebody!*

## Day 28: Faith and Creativity

**Affirmation**: My faith inspires creativity and a unique perspective.

*Exodus 35:31-32 - "And he has filled him with the Spirit of God, with wisdom, with understanding, with knowledge and with all kinds of skills—to make artistic designs for work in gold, silver and bronze."*

**Reflective Question**: How does my faith inspire my creativity?

_____

_____

_____

_____

**My Personal Affirmation for Today:**

_____

_____

_____

_____

*Amen Somebody!*

## Day 29: Faith and Celebration

**Affirmation**: I celebrate my faith and the profound impact it has on my life.

*Psalm 150:6 - "Let everything that has breath praise the Lord. Praise the Lord."*

**Reflective Question**: What aspects of my faith am I most thankful for and wish to celebrate?

_____
_____
_____
_____

**My Personal Affirmation for Today:**

_____
_____
_____
_____

*Amen Somebody!*

# March: 31 Days | Seeking Purpose

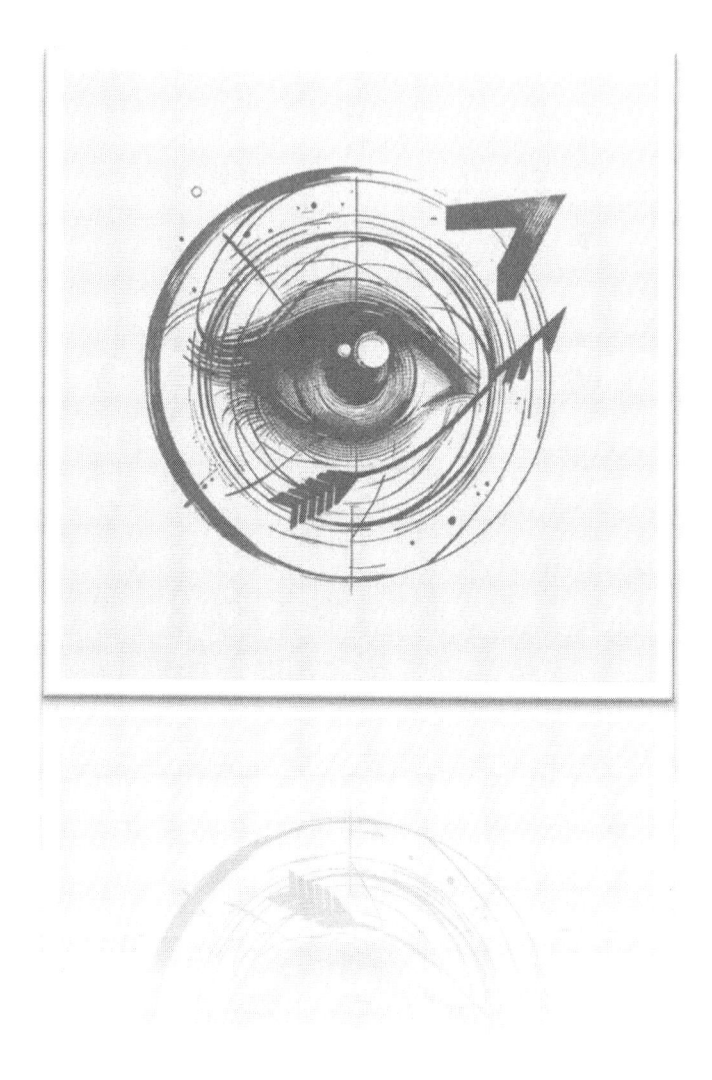

*Amen Somebody!*

## Day 1: Discovering Purpose

**Affirmation**: Every day, I move closer to discovering my true purpose.

*Jeremiah 29:11 - "For I know the plans I have for you," declares the Lord, "plans to prosper you and not to harm you, plans to give you hope and a future."*

**Reflective Question**: What steps can I take today to explore my purpose?

_____
_____
_____
_____

**My Personal Affirmation for Today:**

_____
_____
_____
_____

*Amen Somebody!*

## Day 2: Living Intentionally

**Affirmation**: I live each day with intention and purpose.

*Ephesians 5:15-16 - "Be very careful, then, how you live—not as unwise but as wise, making the most of every opportunity, because the days are evil."*

**Reflective Question**: How did I live intentionally today?

_____

_____

_____

_____

**My Personal Affirmation for Today:**

_____

_____

_____

_____

*Amen Somebody!*

## Day 3: Unique Talents

**Affirmation**: My unique talents and abilities lead me to my purpose.

*1 Peter 4:10 - "Each of you should use whatever gift you have received to serve others, as faithful stewards of God's grace in its various forms."*

**Reflective Question**: What are my unique talents and how can they guide me to my purpose?

_____

_____

_____

_____

**My Personal Affirmation for Today:**

_____

_____

_____

*Amen Somebody!*

## Day 4: Guided by Passion

**Affirmation**: My passions guide me to my divine purpose.

*Psalm 37:4 - "Delight yourself in the Lord, and he will give you the desires of your heart."*

**Reflective Question**: What am I passionate about and how does it relate to my purpose?

_____

_____

_____

**My Personal Affirmation for Today:**

_____

_____

_____

*Amen Somebody!*

## Day 5: Embracing Change

**Affirmation**: I embrace change as it leads me to new paths and purposes.

*Isaiah 43:19 - "See, I am doing a new thing! Now it springs up; do you not perceive it? I am making a way in the wilderness and streams in the wasteland."*

**Reflective Question**: How can embracing change help me find my purpose?

_____
_____
_____
_____

**My Personal Affirmation for Today:**

_____
_____
_____
_____

*Amen Somebody!*

## Day 6: Inner Wisdom

**Affirmation**: I trust my inner wisdom to guide me to my purpose.

*James 1:5 - "If any of you lacks wisdom, you should ask God, who gives generously to all without finding fault, and it will be given to you."*

**Reflective Question**: What is my inner wisdom telling me about my purpose?

_____
_____
_____
_____

**My Personal Affirmation for Today:**

_____
_____
_____
_____

*Amen Somebody!*

## Day 7: Positive Influence

**Affirmation**: I am a positive influence on others, and this guides my purpose.

*Matthew 5:16 - "In the same way, let your light shine before others, that they may see your good deeds and glorify your Father in heaven."*

**Reflective Question**: How can I positively influence others today?

_____

_____

_____

_____

**My Personal Affirmation for Today:**

_____

_____

_____

*Amen Somebody!*

*365 Days Affirmed*

## Day 8: Learning from Challenges

**Affirmation**: Every challenge I face teaches me more about my purpose.

*Romans 5:3-4 - "Not only so, but we also glory in our sufferings, because we know that suffering produces perseverance; perseverance, character; and character, hope."*

**Reflective Question**: What have recent challenges taught me about my purpose?

_____

_____

_____

_____

**My Personal Affirmation for Today:**

_____

_____

_____

_____

*Amen Somebody!*

*Amen Somebody!*

## Day 9: Being Present

**Affirmation**: Being present in each moment helps clarify my purpose.

*Psalm 46:10 - "Be still and know that I am God; I will be exalted among the nations, I will be exalted in the earth."*

**Reflective Question**: How can being more present help me understand my purpose?

_____

_____

_____

_____

**My Personal Affirmation for Today:**

_____

_____

_____

*Amen Somebody!*

## Day 10: Continuous Growth

**Affirmation**: I am committed to continuous growth in my journey to find purpose.

*2 Peter 3:18 - "But grow in the grace and knowledge of our Lord and Savior Jesus Christ. To him be glory both now and forever! Amen."*

**Reflective Question**: In what areas am I growing that could lead me to my purpose?

_____

_____

_____

_____

**My Personal Affirmation for Today:**

_____

_____

_____

*Amen Somebody!*

## Day 11: Serving Others

**Affirmation**: Serving others brings me closer to my true purpose.

*Galatians 5:13 - "You, my brothers and sisters, were called to be free. But do not use your freedom to indulge the flesh; rather, serve one another humbly in love."*

**Reflective Question**: How does serving others help me find my purpose?

_____
_____
_____
_____

**My Personal Affirmation for Today:**

_____
_____
_____
_____

*Amen Somebody!*

## Day 12: Overcoming Fear

**Affirmation**: I overcome fear and doubt to pursue my true purpose.

*2 Timothy 1:7 - "For God has not given us a spirit of fear, but of power and of love and of a sound mind."*

**Reflective Question**: What fears do I need to overcome to pursue my purpose?

_____
_____
_____
_____

**My Personal Affirmation for Today:**

_____
_____
_____
_____

*Amen Somebody!*

*Amen Somebody!*

## Day 13: Gratitude

**Affirmation**: I am grateful for every experience that leads me to my purpose.

*1 Thessalonians 5:18 - "Give thanks in all circumstances; for this is God's will for you in Christ Jesus."*

**Reflective Question**: What am I grateful for today that is guiding me towards my purpose?

_____

_____

_____

_____

**My Personal Affirmation for Today:**

_____

_____

_____

_____

*Amen Somebody!*

## Day 14: Authentic Self

**Affirmation**: Being my authentic self is integral to fulfilling my purpose.

*1 Samuel 16:7 - "But the Lord said to Samuel, 'Do not consider his appearance or his height, for I have rejected him. The Lord does not look at the things people look at. People look at the outward appearance, but the Lord looks at the heart.'"*

**Reflective Question**: How does being authentic lead me to my purpose?

_____

_____

_____

_____

**My Personal Affirmation for Today:**

_____

_____

_____

*Amen Somebody!*

## Day 15: Inspired Actions

**Affirmation**: I take inspired actions towards fulfilling my purpose.

*Philippians 2:13 - "For it is God who works in you to will and to act in order to fulfill his good purpose."*

**Reflective Question**: What inspired action can I take today towards my purpose?

_____

_____

_____

_____

**My Personal Affirmation for Today:**

_____

_____

_____

_____

*Amen Somebody!*

## Day 16: Clarity of Vision

**Affirmation**: I have a clear vision of my purpose and the path to achieve it.

*Habakkuk 2:2 - "Then the Lord replied: 'Write down the revelation and make it plain on tablets so that a herald may run with it.'"*

**Reflective Question**: What is my vision for my purpose?

_____

_____

_____

_____

**My Personal Affirmation for Today:**

_____

_____

_____

*Amen Somebody!*

*Amen Somebody!*

## Day 17: Courage to Pursue

**Affirmation**: I have the courage to pursue my purpose, even when the path is unclear.

*Joshua 1:9 - "Have I not commanded you? Be strong and courageous. Do not be afraid; do not be discouraged, for the Lord your God will be with you wherever you go."*

**Reflective Question**: How can I show courage today in pursuit of my purpose?

_____
_____
_____
_____

**My Personal Affirmation for Today:**

_____
_____
_____
_____

*Amen Somebody!*

## Day 18: Embracing Opportunities

**Affirmation**: I embrace new opportunities that align with my purpose.

*Ecclesiastes 3:1 - "There is a time for everything, and a season for every activity under the heavens."*

**Reflective Question**: What new opportunities can I explore today?

_____

_____

_____

_____

**My Personal Affirmation for Today:**

_____

_____

_____

_____

*Amen Somebody!*

## Day 19: Patience in the Journey

**Affirmation**: I am patient with myself as I explore my purpose.

*Psalm 37:7 - "Be still before the Lord and wait patiently for him; fret not yourself over the one who prospers in his way, over the man who carries out evil devices!"*

**Reflective Question**: How can I practice patience in my journey to find purpose?

_____

_____

_____

_____

**My Personal Affirmation for Today:**

_____

_____

_____

*Amen Somebody!*

*365 Days Affirmed*

## Day 20: Reflective Learning

**Affirmation**: I learn from my past to guide my future purpose.

*Romans 8:28 - "And we know that in all things God works for the good of those who love him, who have been called according to his purpose."*

**Reflective Question**: What lessons from my past are guiding me towards my purpose?

_____

_____

_____

_____

**My Personal Affirmation for Today:**

_____

_____

_____

_____

*Amen Somebody!*

## Day 21: Embracing My Journey

**Affirmation**: I embrace my unique journey towards finding my purpose.

*Psalm 139:14 - "I praise you because I am fearfully and wonderfully made; your works are wonderful; I know that full well."*

**Reflective Question**: How does my unique journey shape my purpose?

_____

_____

_____

_____

**My Personal Affirmation for Today:**

_____

_____

_____

_____

*Amen Somebody!*

## Day 22: Positive Mindset

**Affirmation**: A positive mindset leads me to discover my true purpose.

*Philippians 4:8 - "Finally, brothers and sisters, whatever is true, whatever is noble, whatever is right, whatever is pure, whatever is lovely, whatever is admirable—if anything is excellent or praiseworthy—think about such things."*

**Reflective Question**: How does maintaining a positive mindset help me in finding my purpose?

_____

_____

_____

**My Personal Affirmation for Today:**

_____

_____

_____

*Amen Somebody!*

## Day 23: Trusting the Process

**Affirmation**: I trust the process of discovering my purpose.

*Proverbs 16:3 - "Commit to the Lord whatever you do, and he will establish your plans."*

**Reflective Question**: How can I better trust the process in my journey to purpose?

_____
_____
_____
_____

**My Personal Affirmation for Today:**

_____
_____
_____
_____

*Amen Somebody!*

## Day 24: Inner Peace

**Affirmation**: Finding my purpose brings me inner peace.

*John 14:27 - "Peace I leave with you; my peace I give you. I do not give to you as the world gives. Do not let your hearts be troubled and do not be afraid."*

**Reflective Question**: How does pursuing my purpose bring me peace?

_____

_____

_____

_____

**My Personal Affirmation for Today:**

_____

_____

_____

_____

*Amen Somebody!*

## Day 25: Letting Go of Limitations

**Affirmation**: I let go of limitations and beliefs that hinder my purpose.

*2 Corinthians 5:17 - "Therefore, if anyone is in Christ, the new creation has come: The old has gone, the new is here!"*

**Reflective Question**: What limitations do I need to let go of to fulfill my purpose?

_____

_____

_____

_____

**My Personal Affirmation for Today:**

_____

_____

_____

_____

*Amen Somebody!*

*365 Days Affirmed*

## Day 26: Joy in the Journey

**Affirmation**: I find joy in the journey towards my purpose.

*Romans 12:12 - "Be joyful in hope, patient in affliction, faithful in prayer."*

**Reflective Question**: How can I find joy in the process of discovering my purpose?

_____
_____
_____
_____

**My Personal Affirmation for Today:**

_____
_____
_____
_____

*Amen Somebody!*

## Day 27: Aligning with Values

**Affirmation**: My values guide me to my true purpose.

*Psalm 119:105 - "Your word is a lamp for my feet, a light on my path."*

**Reflective Question**: How do my values align with my purpose?

_____

_____

_____

_____

**My Personal Affirmation for Today:**

_____

_____

_____

*Amen Somebody!*

**Day 28: Open to Guidance**

**Affirmation**: I am open to guidance and signs that lead me to my purpose.

*Proverbs 3:6 - "In all your ways acknowledge him, and he will make straight your paths."*

**Reflective Question**: What signs or guidance have I received recently about my purpose?

_____
_____
_____
_____

**My Personal Affirmation for Today:**

_____
_____
_____
_____

*Amen Somebody!*

## Day 29: Strength in Vulnerability

**Affirmation**: In my vulnerability, I find strength and clarity about my purpose.

*2 Corinthians 12:9 - "But he said to me, 'My grace is sufficient for you, for my power is made perfect in weakness.' Therefore I will boast all the more gladly about my weaknesses, so that Christ's power may rest on me."*

**Reflective Question**: How has vulnerability helped me understand my purpose better?

_____

_____

_____

_____

**My Personal Affirmation for Today:**

_____

_____

_____

*Amen Somebody!*

*365 Days Affirmed*

## Day 30: Celebrating Progress

**Affirmation**: I celebrate every step I take towards finding my purpose.

*Psalm 118:24 - "This is the day the Lord has made; let us rejoice and be glad in it."*

**Reflective Question**: What progress towards my purpose can I celebrate today?

_____
_____
_____
_____

**My Personal Affirmation for Today:**

_____
_____
_____
_____

*Amen Somebody!*

## Day 31: Commitment to Purpose

**Affirmation**: "I am committed to living a life that helps me to pursue my purpose."
*Philippians 3:13- " Brothers and sisters, I do not consider myself yet to have taken hold of it. But one thing I do: Forgetting what is behind and straining toward what is ahead."*

**Reflective Question**: How am I actively aligning my daily choices and actions with my commitment to pursuing my purpose in life?

_____
_____
_____

**My Personal Affirmation for Today:**
_____
_____
_____

*Amen Somebody!*

# April: 30 Days | Love

*Amen Somebody!*

## Day 1: I Choose to Love

**Affirmation:** Today, I open my heart to love in all its forms.

*Corinthians 13:4 - "Love is patient, love is kind. It does not envy, it does not boast, it is not proud."*

**Reflective Question:** How can I show more patience and kindness in my relationships today?

_____

_____

_____

_____

**My Personal Affirmation for Today:**

_____

_____

_____

_____

*Amen Somebody!*

## Day 2: I Am Worthy

**Affirmation:** I am worthy of giving and receiving love.

*1 John 4:19 - "We love because He first loved us."*

**Reflective Question:** In what ways can I remind myself of my worthiness of love today?

_____

_____

_____

_____

**My Personal Affirmation for Today:**

_____

_____

_____

_____

*Amen Somebody!*

## Day 3: Love Surrounds Me

**Affirmation:** Love surrounds me in all aspects of my life.

*1 Peter 4:8 - "Above all, love each other deeply, because love covers over a multitude of sins."*

**Reflective Question:** How can I deepen my love for those around me?

_____
_____
_____
_____

**My Personal Affirmation for Today:**

_____
_____
_____
_____

*Amen Somebody!*

## Day 4: I Will Approach Challenges in Love

**Affirmation:** I choose to approach challenges in my relationships with love and understanding. *Ephesians 4:2 - "Be completely humble and gentle; be patient, bearing with one another in love."*

**Reflective Question:** What challenge can I approach with more gentleness and understanding today?

_____

_____

_____

_____

**My Personal Affirmation for Today:**

_____

_____

_____

_____

*Amen Somebody!*

*Amen Somebody!*

## Day 5: Past Hurt No Longer Bind Me

**Affirmation:** I let go of past hurts and embrace love in the present.

*Proverbs 10:12 - "Hatred stirs up conflict, but love covers over all wrongs."*

**Reflective Question:** What past hurt can I release today to make room for more love in my life?

_____
_____
_____
_____

**My Personal Affirmation for Today:**
_____
_____
_____

*Amen Somebody!*

## Day 6: My Heart is Open to Love

**Affirmation:** My heart is open to giving and receiving love in its purest form.

*1 Corinthians 16:14 - "Let all that you do be done in love."*

**Reflective Question:** How can I ensure that my actions today are driven by pure love?

_____

_____

_____

**My Personal Affirmation for Today:**

_____

_____

_____

*Amen Somebody!*

## Day 7: I am Grateful for Love

**Affirmation:** I am grateful for the love that exists in my life.

*Psalm 107:1 - "Give thanks to the Lord, for he is good; his love endures forever."*

**Reflective Question:** What aspects of love in my life am I most grateful for today?

_____
_____
_____
_____

## My Personal Affirmation for Today:

_____
_____
_____
_____

*Amen Somebody!*

## Day 8: There is Strength in Love

**Affirmation:** I find strength in love, and it guides my actions.

*Galatians 5:22 - "But the fruit of the Spirit is love, joy, peace, forbearance, kindness, goodness, faithfulness."*

**Reflective Question:** How did love guide my decisions and interactions today?

_____

_____

_____

_____

**My Personal Affirmation for Today:**

_____

_____

_____

_____

*Amen Somebody!*

## Day 9: I am a Beacon of Love

**Affirmation:** I am a beacon of love and compassion in the world.

*John 13:34 - "A new command I give you: Love one another. As I have loved you, so you must love one another."*

**Reflective Question:** In what ways can I show more compassion and love to those around me today?

_____
_____
_____
_____

**My Personal Affirmation for Today:**

_____
_____
_____

*Amen Somebody!*

## Day 10: I am Growing in Love

**Affirmation:** Every day, I grow more in love and understanding.

*Colossians 3:14 - "And over all these virtues put on love, which binds them all together in perfect unity."*

**Reflective Question:** What did I learn today that helped me grow in love and understanding?

_____
_____
_____
_____

**My Personal Affirmation for Today:**

_____
_____
_____
_____

*Amen Somebody!*

## Day 11: Love Heals

**Affirmation:** Love heals me and strengthens my relationships.

*Psalm 147:3 - "He heals the brokenhearted and binds up their wounds."*

**Reflective Question:** How has love brought healing into my life recently?

_____

_____

_____

_____

**My Personal Affirmation for Today:**

_____

_____

_____

_____

*Amen Somebody!*

## Day 12: I am Open to Love

**Affirmation:** I am open to love in its most unexpected forms.

*Hebrews 13:2 - "Do not forget to show hospitality to strangers, for by so doing some people have shown hospitality to angels without knowing it."*

**Reflective Question:** How can I be more open to the unexpected forms of love today?

_____
_____
_____
_____

**My Personal Affirmation for Today:**

_____
_____
_____

*Amen Somebody!*

## Day 13: I am a Conduit of Love

**Affirmation:** My capacity to love grows each day.

*Ephesians 3:18 - "And may you have the power to understand, as all God's people should, how wide, how long, how high, and how deep his love is."*

**Reflective Question:** In what ways did I experience or show deep love today?

_____

_____

_____

_____

**My Personal Affirmation for Today:**

_____

_____

_____

_____

*Amen Somebody!*

## Day 14: I am Guided by Love

**Affirmation:** Love guides me in my journey towards personal growth.

*2 Peter 3:18 - "But grow in the grace and knowledge of our Lord and Savior Jesus Christ. To him be glory both now and forever! Amen."*

**Reflective Question:** How does love influence my personal growth today?

_____
_____
_____
_____

**My Personal Affirmation for Today:**
_____
_____
_____
_____

*Amen Somebody!*

## Day 15: I Deserve Love

**Affirmation:** I am deserving of love, and I allow myself to receive it.

*Matthew 7:12 - "So in everything, do to others what you would have them do to you, for this sums up the Law and the Prophets."*

**Reflective Question:** How can I better allow myself to receive love from others?

_____

_____

_____

_____

**My Personal Affirmation for Today:**

_____

_____

_____

*Amen Somebody!*

## Day 16: Love is My Foundation

**Affirmation:** Love is the foundation of all my meaningful connections.

*Ecclesiastes 4:9 - "Two are better than one, because they have a good return for their labor."*

**Reflective Question:** How did love strengthen one of my relationships today?

_____
_____
_____
_____

**My Personal Affirmation for Today:**

_____
_____
_____
_____

*Amen Somebody!*

## Day 17: I am a Magnet of Love

**Affirmation:** I radiate love and it returns to me manifold.

*Luke 6:38 - "Give, and it will be given to you. A good measure, pressed down, shaken together and running over, will be poured into your lap. For with the measure you use, it will be measured to you."*

**Reflective Question:** In what ways did I experience the return of the love I gave out today?

_____

_____

_____

_____

**My Personal Affirmation for Today:**

_____

_____

_____

*Amen Somebody!*

**Day 18: Love Equips Me**

**Affirmation:** Love empowers me to face any challenge.

*Philippians 4:13 - "I can do all this through him who gives me strength."*

**Reflective Question:** How did love give me strength in a challenging situation today?

_____

_____

_____

_____

**My Personal Affirmation for Today:**

_____

_____

_____

_____

*Amen Somebody!*

## Day 19: I Express Love Freely

**Affirmation:** I express love freely and joyfully.

*Nehemiah 8:10 - "The joy of the Lord is your strength."*

**Reflective Question:** How did expressing love bring me joy today?

_____

_____

_____

_____

**My Personal Affirmation for Today:**

_____

_____

_____

*Amen Somebody!*

## Day 20: Love is Kind

**Affirmation:** I am patient and kind in my acts of love.

*Galatians 5:22 - "But the fruit of the Spirit is love, joy, peace, patience, kindness, goodness, faithfulness."*

**Reflective Question:** How did I demonstrate patience and kindness in my interactions today?

_____
_____
_____
_____

**My Personal Affirmation for Today:**

_____
_____
_____
_____

***Amen Somebody!***

## Day 21: Love Brings Me Joy

**Affirmation:** I find joy in the love I share with others.

*Romans 12:12 - "Be joyful in hope, patient in affliction, faithful in prayer."*

**Reflective Question:** How did sharing love bring me joy today?

_____
_____
_____
_____

**My Personal Affirmation for Today:**

_____
_____
_____
_____

*Amen Somebody!*

*365 Days Affirmed*

## Day 22: Love Helps Me Understand Others

**Affirmation:** My heart is open to understanding and empathizing with others.

*1 Peter 3:8 - "Finally, all of you, be like-minded, be sympathetic, love one another, be compassionate and humble."*

**Reflective Question:** How did I show empathy and understanding in my interactions today?

_____

_____

_____

_____

**My Personal Affirmation for Today:**

_____

_____

_____

_____

*Amen Somebody!*

*Amen Somebody!*

## Day 23: My Love Has No Conditions

**Affirmation:** I am a source of unconditional love and acceptance.

*Romans 15:7 - "Accept one another, then, just as Christ accepted you, in order to bring praise to God."*

**Reflective Question:** How can I show more unconditional love and acceptance towards others?

_____

_____

_____

_____

**My Personal Affirmation for Today:**

_____

_____

_____

_____

*Amen Somebody!*

## Day 24: Love Inspires Me to Be Better

**Affirmation:** Love inspires me to be my best self.

*Hebrews 10:24 - "And let us consider how we may spur one another on toward love and good deeds."*

**Reflective Question:** In what ways did love inspire me to be better today?

_____
_____
_____
_____

**My Personal Affirmation for Today:**
_____
_____
_____
_____

*Amen Somebody!*

## Day 25: I am Thankful for Love

**Affirmation:** I am grateful for the love that enriches my life.

*Philippians 1:3 - "I thank my God every time I remember you."*

**Reflective Question:** What aspects of love in my life am I most thankful for today?

_____
_____
_____
_____

**My Personal Affirmation for Today:**

_____
_____
_____
_____

*Amen Somebody!*

## Day 26: Love is as Love Does

**Affirmation:** Love is the driving force behind my actions and decisions.

*Colossians 3:17 - "And whatever you do, whether in word or deed, do it all in the name of the Lord Jesus, giving thanks to God the Father through him."*

**Reflective Question:** How did love influence my actions and decisions today?

_____

_____

_____

_____

**My Personal Affirmation for Today:**

_____

_____

_____

_____

*Amen Somebody!*

## Day 27: I Build in Love

**Affirmation:** I nurture my relationships with love and care.

*1 Thessalonians 5:11 - "Therefore encourage one another and build each other up, just as in fact you are doing."*

**Reflective Question:** How did I nurture a relationship with love and care today?

_____
_____
_____
_____

**My Personal Affirmation for Today:**

_____
_____
_____
_____

*Amen Somebody!*

*365 Days Affirmed*

## Day 28: Love Helps Me over Come Fear

**Affirmation:** Love helps me overcome fears and uncertainties.

*1 John 4:18 - "There is no fear in love. But perfect love drives out fear, because fear has to do with punishment. The one who fears is not made perfect in love."*

**Reflective Question:** How did love help me overcome a fear or uncertainty today?

_____

_____

_____

_____

**My Personal Affirmation for Today:**

_____

_____

_____

_____

***Amen Somebody!***

*Amen Somebody!*

## Day 29: Love Encompasses Me

**Affirmation:** I am committed to fostering love in all areas of my life.

*1 Corinthians 13:13 - "And now these three remain: faith, hope and love. But the greatest of these is love."*

**Reflective Question:** What steps did I take today to foster love in different areas of my life?

_____
_____
_____
_____

**My Personal Affirmation for Today:**

_____
_____
_____
_____

*Amen Somebody!*

## Day 30: Love Leads Me

**Affirmation:** Love is the essence of my being and the foundation of my life.

*1 John 4:16 - "God is love. Whoever lives in love lives in God, and God in them."*

**Reflective Question:** How did I embody the essence of love in my actions and thoughts today?

_____

_____

_____

**My Personal Affirmation for Today:**

_____

_____

_____

*Amen Somebody!*

# May: 31 Days | Learning to Trust God

*365 Days Affirmed*

## Day 1: Embracing Faith

**Affirmation**: Today, I choose to walk in faith, trusting that God is guiding my path.

*Proverbs 3:5-6 - "Trust in the Lord with all your heart and lean not on your own understanding; in all your ways submit to him, and he will make your paths straight."*

**Reflective Question**: What area of my life do I need to trust God with more fully today?

_____
_____
_____
_____


**My Personal Affirmation for Today:**

_____
_____
_____
_____

*Amen Somebody!*

## Day 2: Letting Go of Worry

**Affirmation**: I release my worries and rest in the assurance of God's love and care.

*Philippians 4:6-7 - "Do not be anxious about anything, but in every situation, by prayer and petition, with thanksgiving, present your requests to God."*

**Reflective Question**: How can I replace my worries with prayers and gratitude today?

_____

_____

_____

_____

**My Personal Affirmation for Today:**

_____

_____

_____

_____

***Amen Somebody!***

## Day 3: Strength in Faith

**Affirmation**: My strength is renewed as I put my trust in God.

*Isaiah 40:31 - "But those who hope in the Lord will renew their strength. They will soar on wings like eagles; they will run and not grow weary, they will walk and not be faint."*

**Reflective Question**: When have I felt God renewing my strength in a challenging time?

_____

_____

_____

_____

**My Personal Affirmation for Today:**

_____

_____

_____

_____

*Amen Somebody!*

## Day 4: Peace in Trust

**Affirmation**: In trusting God, I find a peace that surpasses all understanding.

*John 14:27 - "Peace I leave with you; my peace I give you. I do not give to you as the world gives. Do not let your hearts be troubled and do not be afraid."*

**Reflective Question**: What does God's peace mean to me in my current circumstances?

_____

_____

_____

_____

**My Personal Affirmation for Today:**

_____

_____

_____

_____

*Amen Somebody!*

## Day 5: Guided by His Will

**Affirmation**: I am confident that God is leading me according to His perfect will.

*Romans 8:28 - "And we know that in all things God works for the good of those who love him, who have been called according to his purpose."*

**Reflective Question**: How can I align my daily actions with God's will?

_____

_____

_____

_____

**My Personal Affirmation for Today:**

_____

_____

_____

_____

*Amen Somebody!*

## Day 6: Overcoming Fear with Faith

**Affirmation**: By trusting in God, I overcome my fears with faith.

*2 Timothy 1:7 - "For God has not given us a spirit of fear, but of power and of love and of a sound mind."*

**Reflective Question**: What fear do I need to surrender to God today?

_____

_____

_____

_____

## My Personal Affirmation for Today:

_____

_____

_____

_____

*Amen Somebody!*

## Day 7: Trusting in God's Timing

**Affirmation**: I trust in God's perfect timing for every aspect of my life.

*Ecclesiastes 3:11 - "He has made everything beautiful in its time. He has also set eternity in the human heart; yet no one can fathom what God has done from beginning to end."*

**Reflective Question**: How can I practice patience and trust in God's timing today?

_____

_____

_____

_____

**My Personal Affirmation for Today:**

_____

_____

_____

_____

*Amen Somebody!*

## Day 8: Finding Joy in Trust

**Affirmation:** I find joy and contentment in placing my trust in God.

*Nehemiah 8:10 - "The joy of the Lord is your strength."*

**Reflective Question:** How does trusting in God bring joy into my life, even in challenging times?

_____
_____
_____
_____

**My Personal Affirmation for Today:**

_____
_____
_____
_____

*Amen Somebody!*

## Day 9: Surrendering Control

**Affirmation**: I surrender my need for control and trust in God's perfect plan.

*Proverbs 16:9 - "In their hearts humans plan their course, but the Lord establishes their steps."*

**Reflective Question**: What am I trying to control that I need to entrust to God?

_____
_____
_____
_____

**My Personal Affirmation for Today:**

_____
_____
_____
_____

*Amen Somebody!*

## Day 10: Trusting Through Trials

**Affirmation**: Even in trials, I trust that God is working for my good.

*James 1:2-3 - "Consider it pure joy, my brothers and sisters, whenever you face trials of many kinds, because you know that the testing of your faith produces perseverance."*

**Reflective Question**: How can my current trials strengthen my trust in God?

_____
_____
_____
_____

**My Personal Affirmation for Today:**

_____
_____
_____
_____

***Amen Somebody!***

## Day 11: God's Unfailing Love

**Affirmation**: I trust in God's unfailing love and mercy every day.

*Psalm 13:5 - "But I trust in your unfailing love; my heart rejoices in your salvation."*

**Reflective Question**: In what ways have I experienced God's unfailing love recently?

_____

_____

_____

_____

**My Personal Affirmation for Today:**

_____

_____

_____

_____

*Amen Somebody!*

### Day 12: Walking by Faith

**Affirmation**: I choose to walk by faith, not by sight, trusting in God's guidance.

*2 Corinthians 5:7 - "For we live by faith, not by sight."*

**Reflective Question**: What does walking by faith look like in my current situation?

_____
_____
_____
_____

**My Personal Affirmation for Today:**

_____
_____
_____
_____

*Amen Somebody!*

## Day 13: Trust in God's Provision

**Affirmation**: I trust that God will provide for all my needs.

*Matthew 6:31-33 - "So do not worry, saying, 'What shall we eat?' or 'What shall we drink?' or 'What shall we wear?'... But seek first his kingdom and his righteousness, and all these things will be given to you as well."*

**Reflective Question**: How have I seen God provide for my needs in unexpected ways?

_____

_____

_____

_____

**My Personal Affirmation for Today:**

_____

_____

_____

*Amen Somebody!*

## Day 14: Resting in God's Promises

**Affirmation**: I find rest in the promises of God, knowing He is faithful.

*Joshua 21:45 - "Not one of all the Lord's good promises to Israel failed; every one was fulfilled."*

**Reflective Question**: Which of God's promises do I need to hold onto more firmly today?

_____
_____
_____
_____

**My Personal Affirmation for Today:**

_____
_____
_____
_____

*Amen Somebody!*

## Day 15: Courage in the Lord

**Affirmation**: I find courage and strength by placing my trust in the Lord.

*Joshua 1:9 - "Have I not commanded you? Be strong and courageous. Do not be afraid; do not be discouraged, for the Lord your God will be with you wherever you go."*

**Reflective Question**: In what situation do I need to claim God's promise of courage and strength today?

_____

_____

_____

_____

**My Personal Affirmation for Today:**

_____

_____

_____

_____

*Amen Somebody!*

## Day 16: Trusting in Times of Uncertainty

**Affirmation:** In times of uncertainty, I trust that God is with me and for me.

*Psalm 56:3 - "When I am afraid, I put my trust in you."*

**Reflective Question:** How can I remind myself of God's presence in uncertain times?

_____

_____

_____

_____

**My Personal Affirmation for Today:**

_____

_____

_____

_____

*Amen Somebody!*

## Day 17: Faith Over Fear

**Affirmation**: I choose faith over fear, trusting in God's protection and guidance.

*Psalm 91:2 - "I will say of the Lord, 'He is my refuge and my fortress, my God, in whom I trust."*

**Reflective Question**: What fears do I need to replace with faith in God's protection?

_____
_____
_____
_____

**My Personal Affirmation for Today:**

_____
_____
_____
_____

*Amen Somebody!*

## Day 18: Trusting God's Timing

**Affirmation**: I trust in God's perfect timing, knowing He knows what is best for me.
*Psalm 27:14 - "Wait for the Lord; be strong and take heart and wait for the Lord."*
**Reflective Question**: Where do I need to exercise patience and trust in God's timing?

_____
_____
_____
_____

**My Personal Affirmation for Today:**

_____
_____
_____
_____

***Amen Somebody!***

## Day 19: Gratitude in Trust

**Affirmation**: I express gratitude for God's faithfulness and trustworthiness.

*1 Thessalonians 5:18 - "Give thanks in all circumstances; for this is God's will for you in Christ Jesus."*

**Reflective Question**: What recent experiences have deepened my gratitude for God's faithfulness?

_____

_____

_____

_____

**My Personal Affirmation for Today:**

_____

_____

_____

_____

***Amen Somebody!***

## Day 20: Trust and Obedience

**Affirmation**: My trust in God is reflected in my obedience to His word.

*John 14:23 - "Jesus replied, 'Anyone who loves me will obey my teaching. My Father will love them, and we will come to them and make our home with them."*

**Reflective Question**: How does my daily life reflect my trust in and obedience to God?

_____

_____

_____

_____

**My Personal Affirmation for Today:**

_____

_____

_____

_____

*Amen Somebody!*

## Day 21: God's Guidance in Decision Making

**Affirmation**: I trust in God to guide me in all my decisions.

*Proverbs 2:6 - "For the Lord gives wisdom; from his mouth come knowledge and understanding."*

**Reflective Question**: What decision do I need God's wisdom for today?

_____
_____
_____
_____

**My Personal Affirmation for Today:**

_____
_____
_____
_____

*Amen Somebody!*

## Day 22: Embracing God's Plan

**Affirmation**: I embrace God's plan for my life, trusting in His wisdom and goodness.

*Jeremiah 29:11 - "For I know the plans I have for you," declares the Lord, "plans to prosper you and not to harm you, plans to give you hope and a future."*

**Reflective Question**: How can I align myself more closely with God's plan for my life?

_____

_____

_____

_____

**My Personal Affirmation for Today:**

_____

_____

_____

_____

*Amen Somebody!*

## Day 23: Overcoming Challenges with Faith

**Affirmation**: With faith in God, I overcome challenges and grow stronger.

*Romans 8:37 - No, in all these things we are more than conquerors through him who loved us.*

**Reflective Question**: What challenge am I facing that I need to entrust to God's care?

_____
_____
_____
_____

**My Personal Affirmation for Today:**
_____
_____
_____
_____

*Amen Somebody!*

## Day 24: Trusting in God's Unchanging Nature

**Affirmation**: I find comfort in God's unchanging nature in a constantly changing world.

*Hebrews 13:8 - "Jesus Christ is the same yesterday and today and forever."*

**Reflective Question**: How does the unchanging nature of God bring stability to my life?

_____

_____

_____

_____

**My Personal Affirmation for Today:**

_____

_____

_____

_____

*Amen Somebody!*

## Day 25: Finding Strength in God's Presence

**Affirmation**: In God's presence, I find the strength and peace I need.

*Psalm 16:11 - "You make known to me the path of life; in your presence there is fullness of joy; at your right hand are pleasures forevermore."*

**Reflective Question**: How can I seek God's presence more in my daily life?

_____

_____

_____

_____

**My Personal Affirmation for Today:**

_____

_____

_____

_____

*Amen Somebody!*

## Day 26: Trusting God in Relationships

**Affirmation**: I trust God to guide and enrich my relationships.

*Proverbs 3:5-6 - "Trust in the Lord with all your heart and lean not on your own understanding; in all your ways submit to him, and he will make your paths straight."*

**Reflective Question**: How can I apply trust in God to strengthen my relationships?

_____

_____

_____

_____

**My Personal Affirmation for Today:**

_____

_____

_____

_____

*Amen Somebody!*

## Day 27: Faith in Difficult Times

**Affirmation**: Even in difficult times, my faith in God remains unshaken.

*Psalm 46:1 - "God is our refuge and strength, an ever-present help in trouble."*

**Reflective Question**: How has my faith been a source of strength in difficult times?

_____

_____

_____

_____

**My Personal Affirmation for Today:**

_____

_____

_____

_____

*Amen Somebody!*

## Day 28: Celebrating God's Goodness

**Affirmation**: I celebrate and acknowledge the goodness of God in all areas of my life.

*Psalm 107:1 - "Give thanks to the Lord, for he is good; his love endures forever."*

**Reflective Question**: What recent experiences have led me to celebrate God's goodness?

_____
_____
_____
_____

**My Personal Affirmation for Today:**

_____
_____
_____
_____

*Amen Somebody!*

## Day 29: Trusting in God's Healing

**Affirmation**: I trust in God's power to heal, restore, and renew.

*Psalm 147:3 - "He heals the brokenhearted and binds up their wounds."*

**Reflective Question**: In what areas of my life do I need to seek God's healing and restoration?

_____

_____

_____

_____

**My Personal Affirmation for Today:**

_____

_____

_____

_____

****Amen Somebody!***

## Day 30: Confidence in God's Sovereignty

**Affirmation**: I have confidence in God's sovereignty over every aspect of my life.
*Psalm 103:19 - "The Lord has established his throne in heaven, and his kingdom rules over all."*
**Reflective Question**: How does recognizing God's sovereignty impact my daily life and decisions?

_____

_____

_____

_____

**My Personal Affirmation for Today:**

_____

_____

_____

_____

*Amen Somebody!*

## Day 31: Growing in Trust Each Day

**Affirmation**: Each day, I grow in my trust and reliance on God.

*2 Peter 3:18 - "But grow in the grace and knowledge of our Lord and Savior Jesus Christ. To him be glory both now and forever! Amen."*

**Reflective Question**: What are the ways I have grown in my trust in God over this past month?

_____

_____

_____

_____

**My Personal Affirmation for Today:**

_____

_____

_____

_____

*Amen Somebody!*

# June: 30 Days | Use What's in Your Hands

*365 Days Affirmed*

## Day 1: Recognizing Your Gifts

**Affirmation**: Today, I acknowledge and appreciate the unique gifts and talents in my hands.

*1 Peter 4:10 - "Each of you should use whatever gift you have received to serve others, as faithful stewards of God's grace in its various forms."*

**Reflective Question**: What are the unique gifts I possess and how can I use them to serve others?

_____

_____

_____

_____

**My Personal Affirmation for Today:**

_____

_____

_____

*Amen Somebody!*

## Day 2: Embracing Opportunities

**Affirmation**: I am open to and ready for the opportunities that come my way.

*Ecclesiastes 9:10 - "Whatever your hand finds to do, do it with all your might..."*

**Reflective Question**: What opportunity can I seize today with the resources I currently have?

_____
_____
_____
_____

**My Personal Affirmation for Today:**

_____
_____
_____
_____

*Amen Somebody!*

## Day 3: Cultivating What You Have

**Affirmation**: I am committed to cultivating and growing the skills and resources in my possession.

*2 Timothy 1:6 - "For this reason I remind you to fan into flame the gift of God, which is in you..."*

**Reflective Question**: How can I actively work on improving and nurturing my skills and talents today?

_____

_____

_____

_____

**My Personal Affirmation for Today:**

_____

_____

_____

_____

*Amen Somebody!*

## Day 4: Overcoming Limitations

**Affirmation**: I choose to focus on my strengths, not my limitations, using what I have to its fullest potential.

*Philippians 4:13 - "I can do all things through Christ who strengthens me."*

**Reflective Question**: What perceived limitations can I overcome by focusing on my strengths?

_____
_____
_____
_____

**My Personal Affirmation for Today:**

_____
_____
_____
_____

*Amen Somebody!*

## Day 5: Making the Most of Today

**Affirmation**: I will make the most of what I have today, trusting that it is enough for my journey.

*Matthew 6:34 - "Therefore do not worry about tomorrow, for tomorrow will worry about itself. Each day has enough trouble of its own."*

**Reflective Question**: How can I best utilize my current resources and abilities today?

_____

_____

_____

_____

**My Personal Affirmation for Today:**

_____

_____

_____

_____

*Amen Somebody!*

## Day 6: Sharing Your Talents

**Affirmation**: I am willing to share my talents and resources with those around me.

*Luke 6:38 - "Give, and it will be given to you. A good measure, pressed down, shaken together and running over, will be poured into your lap..."*

**Reflective Question**: In what ways can I share my talents and resources with others today?

_____

_____

_____

_____

**My Personal Affirmation for Today:**

_____

_____

_____

*Amen Somebody!*

## Day 7: Trusting in God's Provision

**Affirmation**: I trust that God will multiply what's in my hands when I use it wisely and generously.

*2 Corinthians 9:10 - "Now he who supplies seed to the sower and bread for food will also supply and increase your store of seed and will enlarge the harvest of your righteousness."*

**Reflective Question**: How can I demonstrate trust in God's provision through my actions today?

_____

_____

_____

**My Personal Affirmation for Today:**

_____

_____

_____

*Amen Somebody!*

## Day 8: Valuing Small Beginnings

**Affirmation**: I value and respect small beginnings, knowing they are the foundation for greater things.

*Zechariah 4:10 - "Do not despise these small beginnings, for the Lord rejoices to see the work begin..."*

**Reflective Question**: What small step can I take today towards a bigger goal, using the resources I currently have?

_____

_____

_____

_____

**My Personal Affirmation for Today:**

_____

_____

_____

_____

*Amen Somebody!*

## Day 9: Being Resourceful

**Affirmation**: I am resourceful, making the most of what I have at my disposal.

*Proverbs 12:27 - "The diligent find valuable uses for everything they own..."*

**Reflective Question**: How can I be more resourceful with what I have today?

_____
_____
_____
_____

**My Personal Affirmation for Today:**
_____
_____
_____
_____

*Amen Somebody!*

## Day 10: Embracing Creativity

**Affirmation**: I embrace creativity to innovate and make the best use of my resources.

*Exodus 35:31-32 - "He has filled him with the Spirit of God, with wisdom, with understanding, with knowledge and with all kinds of skills—to make artistic designs..."*

**Reflective Question**: In what ways can I apply creativity to use my talents and resources effectively?

_____

_____

_____

_____

**My Personal Affirmation for Today:**

_____

_____

_____

*Amen Somebody!*

## Day 11: The Power of Diligence

**Affirmation**: Through diligence and hard work, I maximize the potential of what's in my hands. *Proverbs 13:4 - "A sluggard's appetite is never filled, but the desires of the diligent are fully satisfied."*

**Reflective Question**: What diligent action can I take today to make the most of my current situation?

_____

_____

_____

**My Personal Affirmation for Today:**

_____

_____

_____

*Amen Somebody!*

*Amen Somebody!*

## Day 12: Focusing on Solutions

**Affirmation**: I focus on solutions, not problems, using my resources to overcome challenges.

*Philippians 2:4 - "Let each of you look not only to his own interests, but also to the interests of others."*

**Reflective Question**: How can I use what I have to find solutions for the challenges I or others face?

_____

_____

_____

_____

**My Personal Affirmation for Today:**

_____

_____

_____

*Amen Somebody!*

## Day 13: Building with What You Have

**Affirmation**: I am building a meaningful life with the resources and talents in my hands.
*1 Corinthians 3:10 - "By the grace God has given me, I laid a foundation as a wise builder..."*
**Reflective Question**: What am I building in my life right now with the resources I have?

_____
_____
_____

**My Personal Affirmation for Today:**
_____
_____
_____

*Amen Somebody!*

## Day 14: Gratitude for Present Resources

**Affirmation**: I am grateful for the resources and abilities I currently possess.

*1 Thessalonians 5:18 - "Give thanks in all circumstances; for this is God's will for you in Christ Jesus."*

**Reflective Question**: How can I express gratitude for what I have, and how does this change my perspective on my current situation?

_____

_____

_____

_____

**My Personal Affirmation for Today:**

_____

_____

_____

_____

*Amen Somebody!*

*365 Days Affirmed*

## Day 15: Embracing Every Opportunity

**Affirmation**: I embrace every opportunity that comes my way, using my abilities to their fullest. *Galatians 6:10 - "Therefore, as we have opportunity, let us do good to all people..."*

**Reflective Question**: What opportunity can I take advantage of today, and how can I use my current abilities to do good?

_____

_____

_____

_____

**My Personal Affirmation for Today:**

_____

_____

_____

_____

*Amen Somebody!*

## Day 16: Overcoming Obstacles with Faith

**Affirmation**: I overcome obstacles by faith, believing that what I have is enough to triumph. *Mark 11:23 - "Truly I tell you, if anyone says to this mountain, 'Go, throw yourself into the sea,' and does not doubt in their heart but believes that what they say will happen, it will be done for them."*

**Reflective Question**: What obstacle am I facing that I can overcome by using my faith and the resources at hand?

_____

_____

_____

_____

**My Personal Affirmation for Today:**

_____

_____

_____

*Amen Somebody!*

## Day 17: The Wisdom to Utilize Resources

**Affirmation**: I seek and apply wisdom to utilize my resources effectively.

*James 1:5 - "If any of you lacks wisdom, you should ask God, who gives generously to all without finding fault, and it will be given to you."*

**Reflective Question**: In what area of my life do I need wisdom to better utilize my resources?

_____

_____

_____

_____

**My Personal Affirmation for Today:**

_____

_____

_____

_____

*Amen Somebody!*

*Amen Somebody!*

## Day 18: Trusting in God's Provision

**Affirmation**: I trust in God's provision, knowing He equips me with what I need. *Philippians 4:19 - "And my God will meet all your needs according to the riches of his glory in Christ Jesus."*
**Reflective Question**: How have I seen God provide for me in the past, and how does this encourage me to use what I have now?

_____

_____

_____

_____

**My Personal Affirmation for Today:**

_____

_____

_____

_____

*Amen Somebody!*

## Day 19: Boldness in Using Your Talents

**Affirmation**: I am bold and courageous in using my talents for greater purposes.

*2 Timothy 1:7 - "For the Spirit God gave us does not make us timid, but gives us power, love and self-discipline."*

**Reflective Question**: How can I be bolder and more courageous in using my talents today?

_____
_____
_____
_____

**My Personal Affirmation for Today:**

_____
_____
_____
_____

***Amen Somebody!***

## Day 20: The Joy of Sharing

**Affirmation**: I find joy in sharing my resources and talents with others.

*Acts 20:35 - "In everything I did, I showed you that by this kind of hard work we must help the weak, remembering the words the Lord Jesus himself said: 'It is more blessed to give than to receive.'"*

**Reflective Question**: What can I share today, and how does sharing bring me joy?

_____

_____

_____

_____

**My Personal Affirmation for Today:**

_____

_____

_____

_____

*Amen Somebody!*

## Day 21: Perseverance in Developing Your Skills

**Affirmation**: I am committed to persevering in developing and honing my skills.

*Romans 5:3-4 - "Not only so, but we also glory in our sufferings, because we know that suffering produces perseverance; perseverance, character; and character, hope."*

**Reflective Question**: What skill am I currently developing, and how can I demonstrate perseverance in this area?

_____

_____

_____

**My Personal Affirmation for Today:**

_____

_____

_____

*Amen Somebody!*

## Day 22: Recognizing the Value in What You Have

**Affirmation**: I recognize and value the resources and talents I currently possess.

*Ecclesiastes 7:18 - "It is good to grasp the one and not let go of the other. Whoever fears God will avoid all extremes."*

**Reflective Question**: How can I better recognize and value the resources and talents I have?

_____

_____

_____

_____

**My Personal Affirmation for Today:**

_____

_____

_____

*Amen Somebody!*

## Day 23: Being a Blessing to Others

**Affirmation**: I use what I have to be a blessing to others.

*Genesis 12:2 - "I will make you into a great nation, and I will bless you; I will make your name great, and you will be a blessing."*

**Reflective Question**: In what ways can I use my resources and talents to bless others today?

_____
_____
_____
_____

**My Personal Affirmation for Today:**

_____
_____
_____

*Amen Somebody!*

*Amen Somebody!*

## Day 24: The Courage to Start

**Affirmation**: I have the courage to start new ventures with the resources in my hands.

*Deuteronomy 31:6 - "Be strong and courageous. Do not be afraid or terrified because of them, for the Lord your God goes with you; he will never leave you nor forsake you."*

**Reflective Question**: What new venture can I courageously start with what I currently have?

_____

_____

_____

_____

**My Personal Affirmation for Today:**

_____

_____

_____

*Amen Somebody!*

## Day 25: Faithfulness in Small Things

**Affirmation**: I am faithful in small things, knowing they lead to greater responsibilities.

*Luke 16:10 - "Whoever can be trusted with very little can also be trusted with much..."*

**Reflective Question**: How can I demonstrate faithfulness in the small tasks or resources I have today?

_____

_____

_____

_____

**My Personal Affirmation for Today:**

_____

_____

_____

_____

*Amen Somebody!*

## Day 26: The Art of Adaptability

**Affirmation**: I adapt and make the best use of the changing circumstances around me.

*James 4:15 - "Instead, you ought to say, 'If it is the Lord's will, we will live and do this or that."*

**Reflective Question**: How can I adapt to my current circumstances to make the best use of what I have?

_____

_____

_____

_____

**My Personal Affirmation for Today:**

_____

_____

_____

_____

*Amen Somebody!*

## Day 27: Celebrating Progress

**Affirmation**: I celebrate every progress I make by effectively using my resources.

*Philippians 1:6 - "Being confident of this, that he who began a good work in you will carry it on to completion until the day of Christ Jesus."*

**Reflective Question**: What progress have I made recently that I can celebrate today?

_____
_____
_____
_____

**My Personal Affirmation for Today:**

_____
_____
_____
_____

***Amen Somebody!***

*Amen Somebody!*

## Day 28: The Power of a Positive Mindset

**Affirmation**: With a positive mindset, I see the potential in everything I have.

*Romans 12:2 - "Do not conform to the pattern of this world, but be transformed by the renewing of your mind. Then you will be able to test and approve what God's will is—his good, pleasing and perfect will."*

**Reflective Question**: How can a positive mindset help me see and use the potential in my current resources?

_____

_____

_____

**My Personal Affirmation for Today:**

_____

_____

_____

*Amen Somebody!*

## Day 29: Embracing Change with Confidence

**Affirmation**: I embrace change with confidence, knowing that I have what it takes to adapt and thrive.

*Joshua 1:9 - "Have I not commanded you? Be strong and courageous. Do not be afraid; do not be discouraged, for the Lord your God will be with you wherever you go."*

**Reflective Question**: How can I confidently adapt to changes in my life using the resources and talents I possess?

_____

_____

_____

**My Personal Affirmation for Today:**

_____

_____

_____

*Amen Somebody!*

## Day 30: Reflecting on Growth and Potential

**Affirmation**: I reflect on my growth and recognize the untapped potential in what I have. *Ephesians 3:20 - "Now to him who is able to do immeasurably more than all we ask or imagine, according to his power that is at work within us,"*

**Reflective Question**: As I reflect on the past month, how have I grown, and what potential do I see in the resources and talents I have?

_____

_____

_____

_____

**My Personal Affirmation for Today:**

_____

_____

_____

_____

*Amen Somebody!*

*365 Days Affirmed*

# July: 31 Days | Overcoming Rejection

*Amen Somebody!*

## Day 1: Embracing Self-Worth

**Affirmation**: I am valued and loved, regardless of others' opinions or actions.

*Isaiah 43:4 - "Since you are precious and honored in my sight, and because I love you..."*

**Reflective Question**: How can I remind myself of my intrinsic worth today, despite external opinions?

_____

_____

_____

_____

**My Personal Affirmation for Today:**

_____

_____

_____

_____

*Amen Somebody!*

## Day 2: Learning from Rejection

**Affirmation**: Every rejection is an opportunity to learn and grow stronger.

*Romans 5:3-4 - "Not only so, but we also glory in our sufferings, because we know that suffering produces perseverance; perseverance, character; and character, hope."*

**Reflective Question**: What positive lesson can I take away from a recent experience of rejection?

_____

_____

_____

_____

**My Personal Affirmation for Today:**

_____

_____

_____

_____

***Amen Somebody!***

## Day 3: Resilience in the Face of No

**Affirmation**: I am resilient and strong, capable of overcoming any 'no' I encounter.

*Joshua 1:9 - "Have I not commanded you? Be strong and courageous. Do not be afraid; do not be discouraged..."*

**Reflective Question**: How can I demonstrate strength and courage today in a situation where I have felt rejected?

_____
_____
_____
_____

**My Personal Affirmation for Today:**

_____
_____
_____
_____

*Amen Somebody!*

## Day 4: Finding Comfort in God's Love

**Affirmation**: I find comfort and acceptance in God's unconditional love.

*Romans 8:38-39 - "For I am convinced that neither death nor life...will be able to separate us from the love of God that is in Christ Jesus our Lord."*

**Reflective Question**: How does the knowledge of God's unconditional love help me deal with feelings of rejection?

_____
_____
_____
_____

**My Personal Affirmation for Today:**
_____
_____
_____
_____

***Amen Somebody!***

## Day 5: Self-Compassion and Understanding

**Affirmation**: I treat myself with compassion and understanding, acknowledging my feelings without judgment.

*Psalm 34:18 - "The Lord is close to the brokenhearted and saves those who are crushed in spirit."*

**Reflective Question**: How can I show myself compassion today in the same way I would to a good friend?

_____

_____

_____

_____

**My Personal Affirmation for Today:**

_____

_____

_____

_____

*Amen Somebody!*

## Day 6: The Power of Persistence

**Affirmation**: I am persistent and will not be deterred by rejection.

*Galatians 6:9 - "Let us not become weary in doing good, for at the proper time we will reap a harvest if we do not give up."*

**Reflective Question**: What are the ways I can continue to persist in my goals despite facing rejection?

_____

_____

_____

_____

**My Personal Affirmation for Today:**

_____

_____

_____

_____

*Amen Somebody!*

## Day 7: Embracing a Positive Outlook

**Affirmation**: I maintain a positive outlook, knowing that rejection does not define my future.

*Jeremiah 29:11 - "For I know the plans I have for you," declares the Lord, "plans to prosper you and not to harm you, plans to give you hope and a future."*

**Reflective Question**: How can I cultivate a positive outlook today, even in the face of rejection?

_____

_____

_____

_____

**My Personal Affirmation for Today:**

_____

_____

_____

***Amen Somebody!***

*365 Days Affirmed*

## Day 8: Recognizing Personal Growth

**Affirmation**: Each rejection is a steppingstone to my personal growth and success.

*James 1:12 - "Blessed is the one who perseveres under trial because, having stood the test, that person will receive the crown of life that the Lord has promised to those who love him."*

**Reflective Question**: How have I grown personally from my experiences with rejection?

_____
_____
_____
_____

**My Personal Affirmation for Today:**

_____
_____
_____
_____

*Amen Somebody!*

*Amen Somebody!*

## Day 9: Finding Strength in Vulnerability

**Affirmation**: In my vulnerability, I find strength and authenticity.

*2 Corinthians 12:9 - "But he said to me, 'My grace is sufficient for you, for my power is made perfect in weakness."*

**Reflective Question**: How can embracing my vulnerability be a source of strength in dealing with rejection?

_____

_____

_____

_____

**My Personal Affirmation for Today:**

_____

_____

_____

_____

*Amen Somebody!*

*365 Days Affirmed*

## Day 10: Trusting in Divine Timing

**Affirmation**: I trust in God's timing, knowing that every 'no' leads me closer to the right 'yes'. *Ecclesiastes 3:1 - "To everything there is a season, and a time to every purpose under the heaven."*

**Reflective Question**: How can I cultivate trust in divine timing, especially when facing rejection?

_____

_____

_____

_____

**My Personal Affirmation for Today:**

_____

_____

_____

_____

*Amen Somebody!*

## Day 11: Embracing New Beginnings

**Affirmation**: Every rejection opens the door to new beginnings and opportunities.

*Isaiah 43:19 - "See, I am doing a new thing! Now it springs up; do you not perceive it? I am making a way in the wilderness and streams in the wasteland."*

**Reflective Question**: What new beginnings can I embrace today as a result of past rejections?

_____

_____

_____

_____

**My Personal Affirmation for Today:**

_____

_____

_____

_____

*Amen Somebody!*

*365 Days Affirmed*

## Day 12: The Courage to Continue

**Affirmation**: I have the courage to continue, even when faced with rejection.

*Deuteronomy 31:6 - "Be strong and courageous. Do not be afraid or terrified because of them, for the Lord your God goes with you; he will never leave you nor forsake you."*

**Reflective Question**: How can I show courage today in an area where I have previously felt rejected?

_____
_____
_____
_____

**My Personal Affirmation for Today:**

_____
_____
_____

*Amen Somebody!*

## Day 13: Learning to Let Go

**Affirmation**: I learn to let go of what is not meant for me and move forward with grace. *Philippians 3:13-14 - "Brothers and sisters, I do not consider myself yet to have taken hold of it. But one thing I do: Forgetting what is behind and straining toward what is ahead..."*

**Reflective Question**: What do I need to let go of, and how can I move forward with grace?

_____

_____

_____

_____

**My Personal Affirmation for Today:**

_____

_____

_____

_____

*Amen Somebody!*

## Day 14: Self-Belief and Confidence

**Affirmation**: I believe in myself and my abilities, regardless of others' acceptance or rejection.

*1 Samuel 16:7 - "But the Lord said to Samuel, 'Do not consider his appearance or his height, for I have rejected him. The Lord does not look at the things people look at. People look at the outward appearance, but the Lord looks at the heart."*

**Reflective Question**: How can I strengthen my belief in myself and my abilities today?

_____

_____

_____

**My Personal Affirmation for Today:**

_____

_____

_____

*Amen Somebody!*

## Day 15: Valuing Inner Peace

**Affirmation**: I prioritize my inner peace over seeking approval from others.

*John 14:27 - "Peace I leave with you; my peace I give you. I do not give to you as the world gives. Do not let your hearts be troubled and do not be afraid."*

**Reflective Question**: How can I cultivate inner peace today, even in the face of external rejection?

_____

_____

_____

**My Personal Affirmation for Today:**

_____

_____

_____

*Amen Somebody!*

## Day 16: Embracing Self-Expression

**Affirmation**: I express myself authentically and freely, without fear of rejection.

*1 Peter 4:10 - "Each of you should use whatever gift you have received to serve others, as faithful stewards of God's grace in its various forms."*

**Reflective Question**: In what ways can I express my true self more freely today?

_____
_____
_____
_____

**My Personal Affirmation for Today:**

_____
_____
_____
_____

*Amen Somebody!*

## Day 17: Finding Joy in the Journey

**Affirmation**: I find joy in my journey, knowing that each experience shapes me.

*Psalm 30:5 - "Weeping may stay for the night, but rejoicing comes in the morning."*

**Reflective Question**: How can I find joy and learning in the experiences I face today, including rejections?

_____
_____
_____
_____

**My Personal Affirmation for Today:**

_____
_____
_____

*Amen Somebody!*

## Day 18: The Strength to Forgive

**Affirmation**: I possess the strength to forgive those who reject me, freeing myself from bitterness.

*Ephesians 4:31-32 - "Get rid of all bitterness, rage and anger, brawling and slander, along with every form of malice. Be kind and compassionate to one another, forgiving each other, just as in Christ God forgave you."*

**Reflective Question**: Who do I need to forgive for past rejections, and how can this act of forgiveness bring me peace?

_____

_____

_____

**My Personal Affirmation for Today:**

_____

_____

_____

*Amen Somebody!*

## Day 19: Belief in God's Plan

**Affirmation**: I believe in God's plan for me, even when it differs from my own expectations. *Proverbs 19:21 - "Many are the plans in a person's heart, but it is the Lord's purpose that prevails."*

**Reflective Question**: How can I align my expectations with the belief that God's plan for me is perfect, even when facing rejection?

_____

_____

_____

_____

**My Personal Affirmation for Today:**

_____

_____

_____

_____

*Amen Somebody!*

## Day 20: Celebrating Your Uniqueness

**Affirmation**: I celebrate my uniqueness and do not conform to others' expectations.

*Psalm 139:14 - "I praise you because I am fearfully and wonderfully made; your works are wonderful, I know that full well."*

**Reflective Question**: What unique qualities do I possess that I can celebrate today, regardless of others' opinions?

_____

_____

_____

_____

**My Personal Affirmation for Today:**

_____

_____

_____

_____

*Amen Somebody!*

## Day 21: Trusting in Your Journey

**Affirmation**: I trust in my life's journey and believe that every experience has a purpose. *Romans 8:28 - "And we know that in all things God works for the good of those who love him, who have been called according to his purpose."*

**Reflective Question**: How can I trust more deeply in the purpose and direction of my life's journey, especially when faced with rejection?

_____

_____

_____

_____

**My Personal Affirmation for Today:**

_____

_____

_____

_____

*Amen Somebody!*

## Day 22: Embracing Change with Positivity

**Affirmation**: I embrace change positively, knowing that it often leads to new, beneficial paths.

*Isaiah 43:18-19 - "Forget the former things; do not dwell on the past. See, I am doing a new thing! Now it springs up; do you not perceive it?"*

**Reflective Question**: How can I view change, even when spurred by rejection, as a positive step towards something new?

_____

_____

_____

## My Personal Affirmation for Today:

_____

_____

_____

_____

*Amen Somebody!*

## Day 23: The Power of Hope

**Affirmation**: I hold onto hope, knowing that it is a powerful antidote to the fear of rejection. *Romans 15:13 - "May the God of hope fill you with all joy and peace as you trust in him, so that you may overflow with hope by the power of the Holy Spirit."*
**Reflective Question**: How can maintaining hope change my perspective on rejection?

_____

_____

_____

_____

**My Personal Affirmation for Today:**

_____

_____

_____

_____

*Amen Somebody!*

*365 Days Affirmed*

## Day 24: Recognizing Your Worth

**Affirmation**: I recognize my worth and value, independent of others' approval or rejection.

*1 Peter 2:9 - "But you are a chosen people, a royal priesthood, a holy nation, God's special possession, that you may declare the praises of him who called you out of darkness into his wonderful light."*

**Reflective Question**: What are the inherent qualities that define my worth, beyond external validation?

_____

_____

_____

**My Personal Affirmation for Today:**

_____

_____

*Amen Somebody!*

## Day 25: The Courage to Face Fear

**Affirmation**: I have the courage to face my fears of rejection, knowing that each step forward makes me stronger.

*Psalm 27:1 - "The Lord is my light and my salvation—whom shall I fear? The Lord is the stronghold of my life—of whom shall I be afraid?"*

**Reflective Question**: What fears related to rejection can I confront today to grow stronger?

_____

_____

_____

_____

**My Personal Affirmation for Today:**

_____

_____

_____

_____

***Amen Somebody!***

*365 Days Affirmed*

## Day 26: Gratitude in All Circumstances

**Affirmation**: I choose to be grateful in all circumstances, finding lessons and strength in rejection.

*1 Thessalonians 5:18 - "Give thanks in all circumstances; for this is God's will for you in Christ Jesus."*

**Reflective Question**: What aspects of a recent rejection can I be thankful for, and what lessons have I learned?

_____

_____

_____

**My Personal Affirmation for Today:**

_____

_____

_____

_____

*Amen Somebody!*

## Day 27: Embracing Your True Self

**Affirmation**: I embrace and stay true to myself, regardless of others' acceptance.

*Romans 12:2 - "Do not conform to the pattern of this world, but be transformed by the renewing of your mind. Then you will be able to test and approve what God's will is—his good, pleasing and perfect will."*

**Reflective Question**: How can I stay true to myself and my values, even when facing rejection?

_____

_____

_____

_____

**My Personal Affirmation for Today:**

_____

_____

_____

*Amen Somebody!*

*365 Days Affirmed*

## Day 28: The Strength in Perseverance

**Affirmation**: I find strength in perseverance, knowing that persistence builds character and leads to success.

*James 1:4 - "Let perseverance finish its work so that you may be mature and complete, not lacking anything."*

**Reflective Question**: How can persevering through rejection help me grow stronger and more resilient?

_____

_____

_____

_____

**My Personal Affirmation for Today:**

_____

_____

_____

_____

*Amen Somebody!*

## Day 29: Nurturing Self-Confidence

**Affirmation**: I nurture my self-confidence, knowing that my value does not decrease based on someone's inability to see my worth.

*Joshua 1:9 - "Have I not commanded you? Be strong and courageous. Do not be afraid; do not be discouraged, for the Lord your God will be with you wherever you go."*

**Reflective Question**: What steps can I take today to build and nurture my self-confidence?

_____

_____

_____

_____

**My Personal Affirmation for Today:**

_____

_____

_____

_____

*Amen Somebody!*

*365 Days Affirmed*

## Day 30: Finding Strength in Community

**Affirmation**: I find strength and support in my community, reminding me that I am not alone in my experiences.

*Ecclesiastes 4:9-10 - "Two are better than one, because they have a good return for their labor: If either of them falls down, one can help the other up. But pity anyone who falls and has no one to help them up."*

**Reflective Question**: How can my community or support network help me in overcoming feelings of rejection?

_____
_____
_____

**My Personal Affirmation for Today:**

_____
_____
_____

*Amen Somebody!*

## Day 31: Embracing Self-Discovery

**Affirmation**: I embrace the journey of self-discovery that rejection often initiates, finding new depths of strength and resilience within me. *Psalm 139:23-24 - "Search me, God, and know my heart; test me and know my anxious thoughts. See if there is any offensive way in me, and lead me in the way everlasting."*

**Reflective Question**: How has my journey through rejection led to deeper self-discovery and personal growth?

_____

_____

_____


**My Personal Affirmation for Today:**

_____

_____

_____

*Amen Somebody!*

# August: 31 Days | Overcoming Fear

*Amen Somebody!*

## Day 1: Embracing Courage

**Affirmation**: I am filled with courage and strength to face my fears.

*Joshua 1:9 - "Have I not commanded you? Be strong and courageous. Do not be afraid; do not be discouraged, for the Lord your God will be with you wherever you go."*

**Reflective Question**: What fear can I confront today with courage and faith?

_____

_____

_____

_____

**My Personal Affirmation for Today:**

_____

_____

_____

_____

***Amen Somebody!***

## Day 2: Trusting in Divine Protection

**Affirmation**: I trust in God's protection and guidance, which alleviates my fears.

*Psalm 91:1-2 - "Whoever dwells in the shelter of the Most High will rest in the shadow of the Almighty. I will say of the Lord, 'He is my refuge and my fortress, my God, in whom I trust."*

**Reflective Question**: How does trusting in God's protection help me to overcome my fears?

_____
_____
_____
_____

**My Personal Affirmation for Today:**

_____
_____
_____

*Amen Somebody!*

## Day 3: Power, Love, and Self-Discipline

**Affirmation**: I am endowed with power, love, and self-discipline, not a spirit of fear.

*2 Timothy 1:7 - "For God has not given us a spirit of fear, but of power and of love and of a sound mind."*

**Reflective Question**: How can I use power, love, and self-discipline to overcome a specific fear I am facing?

_____

_____

_____

_____

**My Personal Affirmation for Today:**

_____

_____

_____

_____

*Amen Somebody!*

## Day 4: Peace Over Panic

**Affirmation**: I choose peace over panic and trust over trepidation.

*John 14:27 - "Peace I leave with you; my peace I give you. I do not give to you as the world gives. Do not let your hearts be troubled and do not be afraid."*

**Reflective Question**: What steps can I take today to replace panic with peace?

_____
_____
_____
_____

**My Personal Affirmation for Today:**

_____
_____
_____
_____

*Amen Somebody!*

## Day 5: Overcoming Fear with Faith

**Affirmation**: My faith is stronger than my fear.
*Hebrews 11:1 - "Now faith is confidence in what we hope for and assurance about what we do not see."*
**Reflective Question**: How can I demonstrate my faith in an area where fear has been holding me back?

_____
_____
_____
_____

**My Personal Affirmation for Today:**
_____
_____
_____
_____

*Amen Somebody!*

*365 Days Affirmed*

## Day 6: The Strength to Face Challenges

**Affirmation**: I possess the strength to face challenges and overcome my fears.
*Philippians 4:13 - "I can do all this through him who gives me strength."*
**Reflective Question**: What challenge can I tackle today to show my strength over fear?

_____
_____
_____
_____

**My Personal Affirmation for Today:**
_____
_____
_____
_____

*Amen Somebody!*

### Day 7: Embracing the Unknown

**Affirmation**: I embrace the unknown with confidence and curiosity, not fear.

*Jeremiah 29:11 - "For I know the plans I have for you," declares the Lord, "plans to prosper you and not to harm you, plans to give you hope and a future."*

**Reflective Question**: How can I approach the unknown aspects of my life with curiosity and confidence today?

_____

_____

_____

_____

**My Personal Affirmation for Today:**

_____

_____

_____

*Amen Somebody!*

## Day 8: Finding Strength in Vulnerability

**Affirmation**: In my vulnerability, I find strength and courage.

*2 Corinthians 12:9-10 - "But he said to me, 'My grace is sufficient for you, for my power is made perfect in weakness.' Therefore I will boast all the more gladly about my weaknesses, so that Christ's power may rest on me."*

**Reflective Question**: How can acknowledging and embracing my vulnerabilities lead to greater strength and less fear?

_____

_____

_____

**My Personal Affirmation for Today:**

_____

_____

_____

*Amen Somebody!*

*Amen Somebody!*

## Day 9: The Power of Positive Thinking

**Affirmation**: With positive thinking, I transform my fear into opportunity.

*Philippians 4:8 - "Finally, brothers and sisters, whatever is true, whatever is noble, whatever is right, whatever is pure, whatever is lovely, whatever is admirable—if anything is excellent or praiseworthy—think about such things."*

**Reflective Question**: What positive thoughts can I focus on today to overcome fears I am facing?

_____

_____

**My Personal Affirmation for Today:**

_____

_____

*Amen Somebody!*

## Day 10: Embracing Change Fearlessly

**Affirmation**: I embrace change fearlessly, trusting that it leads to growth and new possibilities.

*Isaiah 43:19 - "See, I am doing a new thing! Now it springs up; do you not perceive it? I am making a way in the wilderness and streams in the wasteland."*

**Reflective Question**: How can I view change as a positive and exciting opportunity rather than something to fear?

_____
_____
_____
_____

**My Personal Affirmation for Today:**
_____
_____
_____

***Amen Somebody!***

## Day 11: The Courage to Take Risks

**Affirmation**: I have the courage to take risks and step out of my comfort zone.

*Joshua 1:9 - "Have I not commanded you? Be strong and courageous. Do not be afraid; do not be discouraged, for the Lord your God will be with you wherever you go."*

**Reflective Question**: What risk can I take today to grow beyond my fears?

_____

_____

_____

_____

**My Personal Affirmation for Today:**

_____

_____

_____

_____

*Amen Somebody!*

*365 Days Affirmed*

## Day 12: Trusting in God's Faithfulness

**Affirmation**: I trust in God's faithfulness and promises, which dispel my fears.

*Deuteronomy 31:6 - "Be strong and courageous. Do not be afraid or terrified because of them, for the Lord your God goes with you; he will never leave you nor forsake you."*

**Reflective Question**: How does remembering God's faithfulness in the past help me to trust Him and not be afraid in the present?

_____

_____

_____

**My Personal Affirmation for Today:**

_____

_____

_____

_____

*Amen Somebody!*

## Day 13: Overcoming Fear with Gratitude

**Affirmation**: I overcome fear by focusing on gratitude for the blessings in my life.

*1 Thessalonians 5:18 - "Give thanks in all circumstances; for this is God's will for you in Christ Jesus."*

**Reflective Question**: What am I grateful for today, and how does this gratitude help reduce my fears?

_____

_____

_____

_____

**My Personal Affirmation for Today:**

_____

_____

_____

_____

*Amen Somebody!*

## Day 14: The Freedom of Letting Go

**Affirmation**: I find freedom in letting go of what I cannot control.

*Psalm 46:10 - "Be still, and know that I am God; I will be exalted among the nations, I will be exalted in the earth."*

**Reflective Question**: What fears can I release today by acknowledging that some things are beyond my control?

_____
_____
_____
_____


**My Personal Affirmation for Today:**

_____
_____
_____
_____

*Amen Somebody!*

## Day 15: Celebrating Small Victories

**Affirmation**: I celebrate every small victory over my fears.

*Zechariah 4:10 - "Who dares despise the day of small things..."*

**Reflective Question**: What small victory over fear can I celebrate today?

_____

_____

_____

_____

**My Personal Affirmation for Today:**

_____

_____

_____

_____

***Amen Somebody!***

## Day 16: The Wisdom in Fear

**Affirmation**: I seek wisdom in my fears, understanding they are opportunities for growth. *James 1:5 - "If any of you lacks wisdom, you should ask God, who gives generously to all without finding fault, and it will be given to you."*

**Reflective Question**: What can my current fears teach me, and how can I grow from them?

_____
_____
_____
_____

**My Personal Affirmation for Today:**

_____
_____
_____
_____

*Amen Somebody!*

## Day 17: The Power of Prayer

**Affirmation**: Through prayer, I gain strength and courage to overcome my fears.

*Philippians 4:6-7 - "Do not be anxious about anything, but in every situation, by prayer and petition, with thanksgiving, present your requests to God."*

**Reflective Question**: How can prayer help me in addressing and overcoming my fears today?

_____
_____
_____
_____

**My Personal Affirmation for Today:**

_____
_____
_____
_____

*Amen Somebody!*

## Day 18: Embracing God's Peace

**Affirmation**: I embrace the peace of God, which transcends all understanding and calms my fears. *John 14:27 - "Peace I leave with you; my peace I give you. I do not give to you as the world gives. Do not let your hearts be troubled and do not be afraid."*

**Reflective Question**: How can I allow God's peace to calm my current fears?

_____
_____
_____
_____


**My Personal Affirmation for Today:**

_____
_____
_____
_____

*Amen Somebody!*

## Day 19: The Courage to Face Tomorrow

**Affirmation**: I have the courage to face tomorrow, knowing that God is with me.
*Matthew 6:34 - "Therefore do not worry about tomorrow, for tomorrow will worry about itself. Each day has enough trouble of its own."*
**Reflective Question**: How can I focus on today's strength and courage, without fearing tomorrow?

_____

_____

_____

_____

**My Personal Affirmation for Today:**

_____

_____

_____

_____

***Amen Somebody!***

*365 Days Affirmed*

## Day 20: Finding Joy in the Midst of Fear

**Affirmation**: I find joy and contentment, even when faced with fears.

*Nehemiah 8:10 - "The joy of the Lord is your strength."*

**Reflective Question**: How can I find joy in my life today, despite any fears I may be facing?

_____

_____

_____

_____

**My Personal Affirmation for Today:**

_____

_____

_____

_____

*****Amen Somebody!*****

## Day 21: The Strength in Community

**Affirmation**: I find strength and support in my community to overcome my fears.

*Ecclesiastes 4:12* - *"Though one may be overpowered, two can defend themselves. A cord of three strands is not quickly broken."*

**Reflective Question**: How can my community or support network help me in overcoming my fears?

_____
_____
_____
_____

**My Personal Affirmation for Today:**

_____
_____
_____
_____

*Amen Somebody!*

## Day 22: Trusting in God's Timing

**Affirmation**: I trust in God's perfect timing, releasing my fears about the future.

*Ecclesiastes 3:11* - *"He has made everything beautiful in its time. He has also set eternity in the human heart; yet no one can fathom what God has done from beginning to end."*

**Reflective Question**: How can I practice patience and trust in God's timing to alleviate my fears about what lies ahead?

_____

_____

_____

_____

**My Personal Affirmation for Today:**

_____

_____

_____

*Amen Somebody!*

## Day 23: Overcoming Fear with Love

**Affirmation**: I overcome fear with the power of love and compassion.

*1 John 4:18 - "There is no fear in love. But perfect love drives out fear, because fear has to do with punishment. The one who fears is not made perfect in love."*

**Reflective Question**: How can showing love and compassion to others and myself help in overcoming my fears?

_____

_____

_____

_____

**My Personal Affirmation for Today:**

_____

_____

_____

*Amen Somebody!*

*365 Days Affirmed*

## Day 24: The Courage to Speak Up

**Affirmation**: I have the courage to speak my truth, even in the face of fear.

*Proverbs 31:8 - "Speak up for those who cannot speak for themselves, for the rights of all who are destitute."*

**Reflective Question**: What truth do I need to speak today, and how can I find the courage to do so despite my fears?

_____
_____
_____
_____

**My Personal Affirmation for Today:**

_____
_____
_____
_____

*Amen Somebody!*

## Day 25: Embracing Life's Challenges

**Affirmation**: I embrace life's challenges, knowing they are opportunities for growth. *James 1:2-3 - "Consider it pure joy, my brothers and sisters, whenever you face trials of many kinds, because you know that the testing of your faith produces perseverance."*

**Reflective Question**: What challenge am I currently facing, and how can I view it as an opportunity to grow beyond my fears?

_____

_____

_____

_____

**My Personal Affirmation for Today:**

_____

_____

_____

*Amen Somebody!*

*365 Days Affirmed*

## Day 26: The Power of God's Word

**Affirmation**: I find strength and courage in God's word to overcome my fears.

*Psalm 119:105 - "Your word is a lamp for my feet, a light on my path."*

**Reflective Question**: How can God's word guide me today in overcoming fears I am facing?

_____
_____
_____
_____

**My Personal Affirmation for Today:**

_____
_____
_____
_____

*Amen Somebody!*

## Day 27: The Freedom of Forgiveness

**Affirmation:** I embrace the freedom that comes with forgiveness, releasing any fears tied to past hurts.

*Colossians 3:13 - "Bear with each other and forgive one another if any of you has a grievance against someone. Forgive as the Lord forgave you."*

**Reflective Question:** How can forgiving others and myself help in releasing fears connected to past experiences?

_____

_____

_____

_____

**My Personal Affirmation for Today:**

_____

_____

_____

*Amen Somebody!*

## Day 28: The Joy of Being Present

**Affirmation**: I find joy in being present, not allowing fears of the past or future to hold me back.

*Matthew 6:34 - "Therefore do not worry about tomorrow, for tomorrow will worry about itself. Each day has enough trouble of its own."*

**Reflective Question**: How can I focus on being present today, letting go of fears from the past and worries about the future?

_____

_____

_____

**My Personal Affirmation for Today:**

_____

_____

_____

_____

*Amen Somebody!*

## Day 29: Recognizing God's Presence

**Affirmation**: I am aware of God's presence in my life, which diminishes my fears.

*Psalm 23:4 - "Even though I walk through the darkest valley, I will fear no evil, for you are with me; your rod and your staff, they comfort me."*

**Reflective Question**: How does recognizing God's presence in my daily life help me to feel less fearful?

_____

_____

_____

_____

**My Personal Affirmation for Today:**

_____

_____

_____

_____

*Amen Somebody!*

*365 Days Affirmed*

## Day 30: The Strength to Overcome

**Affirmation**: I am stronger than my fears and capable of overcoming them.

*Isaiah 41:10 - "So do not fear, for I am with you; do not be dismayed, for I am your God. I will strengthen you and help you; I will uphold you with my righteous right hand."*

**Reflective Question**: What strengths do I possess that can help me overcome the fears I face?

_____

_____

_____

**My Personal Affirmation for Today:**

_____

_____

_____

_____

*Amen Somebody!*

## Day 31: Embracing a Hopeful Future

**Affirmation**: I look towards the future with hope and optimism, free from the shackles of fear.

*Jeremiah 29:11 - "For I know the plans I have for you," declares the Lord, "plans to prosper you and not to harm you, plans to give you hope and a future."*

**Reflective Question**: How can I cultivate a hopeful and optimistic outlook for my future, letting go of fears that hold me back?

_____

_____

_____

**My Personal Affirmation for Today:**

_____

_____

_____

_____

***Amen Somebody!***

# September: 30 Days | The Voice of God

*Amen Somebody!*

## Day 1: Opening Your Heart

**Affirmation**: I open my heart to hear God's voice in my life.

*1 Samuel 3:10 - "The Lord came and stood there, calling as at the other times, 'Samuel! Samuel!' Then Samuel said, 'Speak, for your servant is listening.'"*

**Reflective Question**: How can I make space in my day to listen more attentively for God's voice?

_____
_____
_____
_____

**My Personal Affirmation for Today:**

_____
_____
_____
_____

*Amen Somebody!*

*365 Days Affirmed*

## Day 2: Seeking Divine Guidance

**Affirmation**: I seek God's guidance in all aspects of my life.

*Proverbs 3:6 - "In all your ways submit to him, and he will make your paths straight."*

**Reflective Question**: What area of my life currently needs God's guidance the most?

_____
_____
_____

**My Personal Affirmation for Today:**

_____
_____
_____

*Amen Somebody!*

## Day 3: Trusting in God's Timing

**Affirmation**: I trust in God's perfect timing and divine plan.

*Ecclesiastes 3:1 - "To everything there is a season, and a time to every purpose under the heaven."*

**Reflective Question**: How can I cultivate patience and trust in God's timing today?

_____

_____

_____

_____

**My Personal Affirmation for Today:**

_____

_____

_____

_____

*Amen Somebody!*

## Day 4: Finding Peace in God's Presence

**Affirmation**: I find peace and clarity when I rest in God's presence.

*Psalm 46:10 - "Be still, and know that I am God; I will be exalted among the nations, I will be exalted in the earth."*

**Reflective Question**: What steps can I take to find stillness and peace in God's presence today?

_____

_____

_____

**My Personal Affirmation for Today:**

_____

_____

_____

***Amen Somebody!***

## Day 5: Embracing God's Wisdom

**Affirmation**: I embrace the wisdom that comes from God, knowing it guides me rightly.

*James 1:5 - "If any of you lacks wisdom, you should ask God, who gives generously to all without finding fault, and it will be given to you."*

**Reflective Question**: In what situation do I need to seek God's wisdom right now?

_____

_____

_____

_____

**My Personal Affirmation for Today:**

_____

_____

_____

_____

*Amen Somebody!*

## Day 6: Recognizing God's Voice

**Affirmation**: I am attuned to recognizing God's voice in my life.

*John 10:27 - "My sheep listen to my voice; I know them, and they follow me."*

**Reflective Question**: How can I differentiate God's voice from the noise of the world?

_____
_____
_____
_____

**My Personal Affirmation for Today:**
_____
_____
_____
_____

*Amen Somebody!*

## Day 7: Gratitude for Divine Guidance

**Affirmation**: I am grateful for the divine guidance I receive in my life.

*Psalm 107:1 - "Give thanks to the Lord, for he is good; his love endures forever."*

**Reflective Question**: What recent guidance have I received that I am thankful for?

_____
_____
_____
_____

**My Personal Affirmation for Today:**

_____
_____
_____
_____

*Amen Somebody!*

*365 Days Affirmed*

## Day 8: Surrendering to Divine Will

**Affirmation**: I surrender my plans to God's will, trusting in His divine wisdom.

*Proverbs 19:21 - "Many are the plans in a person's heart, but it is the Lord's purpose that prevails."*

**Reflective Question**: In what areas of my life do I need to surrender more fully to God's will?

_____

_____

_____

**My Personal Affirmation for Today:**

_____

_____

_____

*Amen Somebody!*

## Day 9: Seeking Solitude for Clarity

**Affirmation**: In moments of solitude, I find clarity and direction from God.

*Mark 1:35 - "Very early in the morning, while it was still dark, Jesus got up, left the house and went off to a solitary place, where he prayed."*

**Reflective Question**: How can I create moments of solitude to better hear God's voice?

_____

_____

_____

_____

**My Personal Affirmation for Today:**

_____

_____

_____

_____

*Amen Somebody!*

## Day 10: Embracing God's Unfailing Love

**Affirmation**: I am embraced by God's unfailing love and listen for His guidance in that assurance.

*Psalm 13:5 - "But I trust in your unfailing love; my heart rejoices in your salvation."*

**Reflective Question**: How does the knowledge of God's unfailing love influence the way I listen for His guidance?

_____

_____

_____

_____

**My Personal Affirmation for Today:**

_____

_____

_____

_____

*Amen Somebody!*

## Day 11: The Courage to Follow God's Path

**Affirmation**: I have the courage to follow the path God lays before me.

*Psalm 23:4 - "Even though I walk through the darkest valley, I will fear no evil, for you are with me; your rod and your staff, they comfort me."*

**Reflective Question**: What fears do I need to overcome to follow the path God is showing me?

_____
_____
_____
_____

**My Personal Affirmation for Today:**

_____
_____
_____
_____

*Amen Somebody!*

*365 Days Affirmed*

## Day 12: Openness to Divine Teachings

**Affirmation**: I am open and receptive to the teachings and wisdom God imparts.

*Psalm 25:4-5 - "Show me your ways, Lord, teach me your paths. Guide me in your truth and teach me, for you are God my Savior, and my hope is in you all day long."*

**Reflective Question**: What teachings or wisdom am I currently seeking from God?

_____

_____

_____

_____

**My Personal Affirmation for Today:**

_____

_____

_____

_____

*Amen Somebody!*

## Day 13: The Joy of God's Presence

**Affirmation**: I find joy and contentment in the presence of God.

*Psalm 16:11 - "You make known to me the path of life; in your presence there is fullness of joy; at your right hand are pleasures forevermore."*

**Reflective Question**: How do I experience joy in God's presence, and how can I cultivate this joy daily?

_____

_____

_____

_____

**My Personal Affirmation for Today:**

_____

_____

_____

_____

***Amen Somebody!***

## Day 14: Trusting in God's Plan

**Affirmation**: I trust in God's plan, knowing it is designed for my ultimate good.

*Jeremiah 29:11 - "For I know the plans I have for you," declares the Lord, "plans to prosper you and not to harm you, plans to give you hope and a future."*

**Reflective Question**: How can I strengthen my trust in God's plan, especially in times of uncertainty?

_____

_____

_____

_____

**My Personal Affirmation for Today:**

_____

_____

_____

_____

*Amen Somebody!*

## Day 15: Patience in Hearing God

**Affirmation**: I am patient, knowing that God speaks in His own time and way.

*Lamentations 3:25 - "The Lord is good to those who wait for him, to the soul who seeks him."*

**Reflective Question**: How can I practice patience today while waiting to hear God's voice?

_____

_____

_____

_____

**My Personal Affirmation for Today:**

_____

_____

_____

_____

*Amen Somebody!*

## Day 16: Recognizing God in Everyday Life

**Affirmation**: I recognize and acknowledge God's presence in every aspect of my life.

*Acts 17:28 - "For in him we live and move and have our being."*

**Reflective Question**: What are some everyday moments where I can more clearly recognize God's presence?

_____
_____
_____
_____

**My Personal Affirmation for Today:**

_____
_____
_____
_____

*Amen Somebody!*

## Day 17: The Power of God's Word

**Affirmation**: God's word is a lamp to my feet and a light to my path, guiding me always.
*Psalm 119:105 - "Your word is a lamp for my feet, a light on my path."*
**Reflective Question**: How does God's word guide me in my daily decisions and challenges?

_____
_____
_____
_____

**My Personal Affirmation for Today:**

_____
_____
_____
_____

*Amen Somebody!*

## Day 18: Seeking God's Kingdom First

**Affirmation**: I seek God's kingdom first, trusting all else will be provided.

*Matthew 6:33 - "But seek first his kingdom and his righteousness, and all these things will be given to you as well."*

**Reflective Question**: How can I prioritize seeking God's kingdom in my daily life?

_____

_____

_____

_____

**My Personal Affirmation for Today:**

_____

_____

_____

_____

*Amen Somebody!*

## Day 19: The Peace of God's Assurance

**Affirmation**: I am comforted and at peace, knowing God is always with me.

*Isaiah 41:10 - "So do not fear, for I am with you; do not be dismayed, for I am your God. I will strengthen you and help you; I will uphold you with my righteous right hand."*

**Reflective Question**: In what ways have I experienced God's comforting presence recently?

_____

_____

_____

_____

**My Personal Affirmation for Today:**

_____

_____

_____

*Amen Somebody!*

## Day 20: Embracing God's Unchanging Nature

**Affirmation**: I find solace in God's unchanging nature amidst the changes of life.

*Hebrews 13:8 - "Jesus Christ is the same yesterday and today and forever."*

**Reflective Question**: How does the unchanging nature of God provide stability in my life?

_____
_____
_____
_____

**My Personal Affirmation for Today:**

_____
_____
_____
_____

*Amen Somebody!*

## Day 21: The Wisdom of Silence

**Affirmation**: In silence, I find wisdom and hear God's gentle whisper.

*1 Kings 19:12 - "After the earthquake came a fire, but the Lord was not in the fire. And after the fire came a gentle whisper."*

**Reflective Question**: How can I incorporate moments of silence into my day to better hear God's voice?

_____

_____

_____

_____

**My Personal Affirmation for Today:**

_____

_____

_____

_____

*Amen Somebody!*

## Day 22: The Clarity of God's Guidance

**Affirmation**: I trust in the clarity and certainty of God's guidance in my life.

*Proverbs 16:9 - "In their hearts humans plan their course, but the Lord establishes their steps."*

**Reflective Question**: How can I discern and trust in the clarity of God's guidance today?

_____
_____
_____
_____

**My Personal Affirmation for Today:**
_____
_____
_____
_____

***Amen Somebody!***

## Day 23: The Strength of Faith

**Affirmation**: My faith strengthens me to listen and follow God's direction.

*Hebrews 11:1 - "Now faith is confidence in what we hope for and assurance about what we do not see."*

**Reflective Question**: How does my faith empower me to listen more intently to God's voice?

_____
_____
_____
_____

**My Personal Affirmation for Today:**

_____
_____
_____
_____

*Amen Somebody!*

## Day 24: Gratitude for Divine Communication

**Affirmation**: I am grateful for the ways God communicates with me, both big and small.
*Psalm 9:1 - "I will give thanks to you, Lord, with all my heart; I will tell of all your wonderful deeds."*
**Reflective Question**: What recent communications from God am I thankful for?

_____
_____
_____
_____

**My Personal Affirmation for Today:**

_____
_____
_____
_____

### *Amen Somebody!*

## Day 25: The Courage to Act on God's Word

**Affirmation**: I have the courage to act on the word and guidance I receive from God.

*Joshua 1:9 - "Have I not commanded you? Be strong and courageous. Do not be afraid; do not be discouraged, for the Lord your God will be with you wherever you go."*

**Reflective Question**: What action can I take today in response to God's guidance?

_____

_____

_____

_____

**My Personal Affirmation for Today:**

_____

_____

_____

_____

*Amen Somebody!*

## Day 26: Embracing God's Promises

**Affirmation**: I embrace and hold onto the promises God has made to me.

*2 Peter 1:4 - "Through these he has given us his very great and precious promises, so that through them you may participate in the divine nature."*

**Reflective Question**: Which of God's promises am I holding onto today?

_____
_____
_____
_____

**My Personal Affirmation for Today:**
_____
_____
_____
_____

*Amen Somebody!*

## Day 27: The Joy of Spiritual Growth

**Affirmation**: I find joy in the spiritual growth that comes from listening to God.

*Psalm 92:12 - "The righteous will flourish like a palm tree, they will grow like a cedar of Lebanon."*

**Reflective Question**: How has listening to God contributed to my spiritual growth?

_____

_____

_____

_____

**My Personal Affirmation for Today:**

_____

_____

_____

_____

*Amen Somebody!*

## Day 28: Trusting in God's Protection

**Affirmation**: I trust in God's protection as I follow His guidance.

*Psalm 121:7-8 - "The Lord will keep you from all harm—he will watch over your life; the Lord will watch over your coming and going both now and forevermore."*

**Reflective Question**: How does trusting in God's protection give me confidence in following His guidance?

_____

_____

_____

_____

**My Personal Affirmation for Today:**

_____

_____

_____

_____

*Amen Somebody!*

## Day 29: Valuing God's Presence in Silence

**Affirmation**: In the silence, I value and seek God's presence and guidance.

*Psalm 62:5 - "Yes, my soul, find rest in God; my hope comes from him."*

**Reflective Question**: How can I better appreciate and utilize moments of silence to connect with God?

_____
_____
_____
_____

**My Personal Affirmation for Today:**

_____
_____
_____
_____

*Amen Somebody!*

## Day 30: Commitment to Ongoing Spiritual Listening

**Affirmation**: I commit to a lifelong journey of listening to God's voice and guidance.

*Psalm 25:4-5 - "Show me your ways, Lord, teach me your paths. Guide me in your truth and teach me, for you are God my Savior, and my hope is in you all day long."*

**Reflective Question**: What steps can I take to ensure that listening to God remains a central part of my spiritual journey?

_____
_____
_____

**My Personal Affirmation for Today:**

_____
_____
_____
_____

*Amen Somebody!*

# October: 31 Days | Healing

*365 Days Affirmed*

## Day 1: Embracing Healing

**Affirmation**: I am open to the healing power at work in my life.

*Jeremiah 17:14 - "Heal me, O Lord, and I will be healed; save me and I will be saved, for you are the one I praise."*

**Reflective Question**: In what areas of my life am I seeking healing, and how can I open myself more to God's healing power?

_____

_____

_____

_____

**My Personal Affirmation for Today:**

_____

_____

_____

_____

*Amen Somebody!*

## Day 2: Trusting in God's Restoration

**Affirmation**: I trust in God's promise to restore my health and heal my wounds.

*Jeremiah 30:17 - "But I will restore you to health and heal your wounds,' declares the Lord."*

**Reflective Question**: How can I cultivate trust in God's promise of restoration and healing?

_____
_____
_____
_____

**My Personal Affirmation for Today:**

_____
_____
_____
_____

*Amen Somebody!*

## Day 3: The Peace of God's Presence

**Affirmation**: In God's presence, I find peace and comfort in my healing journey.
*Philippians 4:7 - "And the peace of God, which transcends all understanding, will guard your hearts and your minds in Christ Jesus."*
**Reflective Question**: What steps can I take today to feel the peace and comfort of God's presence?

_____

_____

_____

_____


**My Personal Affirmation for Today:**

_____

_____

_____

_____

*Amen Somebody!*

## Day 4: Strength in Weakness

**Affirmation**: In my weakness, God's strength is made perfect and brings healing.

*2 Corinthians 12:9 - "But he said to me, 'My grace is sufficient for you, for my power is made perfect in weakness."*

**Reflective Question**: How can I see my weaknesses as opportunities for God's strength and healing to manifest?

_____
_____
_____
_____

**My Personal Affirmation for Today:**

_____
_____
_____
_____

****Amen Somebody!***

**Day 5: Hope in Healing**

**Affirmation**: I hold onto hope, knowing that healing is a journey with God.

*Romans 12:12 - "Be joyful in hope, patient in affliction, faithful in prayer."*

**Reflective Question**: How can maintaining hope positively impact my healing process?

_____
_____
_____
_____

**My Personal Affirmation for Today:**

_____
_____
_____
_____

*Amen Somebody!*

## Day 6: Gratitude in the Process

**Affirmation**: I am grateful for every step of my healing journey.

*1 Thessalonians 5:18 - "Give thanks in all circumstances; for this is God's will for you in Christ Jesus."*

**Reflective Question**: What aspects of my healing journey can I be thankful for today?

_____
_____
_____
_____

**My Personal Affirmation for Today:**

_____
_____
_____
_____

*Amen Somebody!*

## Day 7: The Comfort of God's Love

**Affirmation**: I am comforted and healed by the endless love of God.

*Psalm 147:3 - "He heals the brokenhearted and binds up their wounds."*

**Reflective Question**: How does the knowledge of God's love bring comfort to me in times of need?

_____

_____

_____

_____

**My Personal Affirmation for Today:**

_____

_____

_____

_____

*Amen Somebody!*

## Day 8: Healing Through Forgiveness

**Affirmation**: I embrace healing that comes from the power of forgiveness.

*Ephesians 4:32 - "Be kind and compassionate to one another, forgiving each other, just as in Christ God forgave you."*

**Reflective Question**: Who do I need to forgive today to aid in my healing journey?

_____

_____

_____

_____

**My Personal Affirmation for Today:**

_____

_____

_____

_____

*Amen Somebody!*

## Day 9: Renewal of Mind and Spirit

**Affirmation**: Each day, I am renewed in mind and spirit, moving closer to complete healing. *Romans 12:2 - "Do not conform to the pattern of this world, but be transformed by the renewing of your mind."*
**Reflective Question**: What steps can I take today to renew my mind and spirit?

_____
_____
_____
_____

**My Personal Affirmation for Today:**
_____
_____
_____
_____

*Amen Somebody!*

## Day 10: The Power of Prayer in Healing

**Affirmation**: I believe in the power of prayer to bring healing and restoration.

*James 5:16 - "The prayer of a righteous person is powerful and effective."*

**Reflective Question**: How can I incorporate prayer more effectively into my daily routine for healing?

_____
_____
_____
_____

**My Personal Affirmation for Today:**

_____
_____
_____
_____

*Amen Somebody!*

*365 Days Affirmed*

## Day 11: Finding Strength in Community

**Affirmation**: I find strength and support in my community, aiding my healing.

*Galatians 6:2 - "Carry each other's burdens, and in this way you will fulfill the law of Christ."*

**Reflective Question**: How can my community support me in my healing process?

_____
_____
_____
_____

**My Personal Affirmation for Today:**

_____
_____
_____
_____

*Amen Somebody!*

*Amen Somebody!*

## Day 12: Embracing God's Timing

**Affirmation**: I trust in God's perfect timing for my healing.

*Ecclesiastes 3:1 - "To everything there is a season, and a time to every purpose under the heaven."*

**Reflective Question**: How can I cultivate patience and trust in God's timing for my healing?

_____

_____

_____

_____

**My Personal Affirmation for Today:**

_____

_____

_____

_____

*Amen Somebody!*

## Day 13: The Joy of God's Healing

**Affirmation**: I find joy in the journey of healing, trusting in God's plan.

*Psalm 30:2 - "Lord my God, I called to you for help, and you healed me."*

**Reflective Question**: What joyful moments have I experienced in my healing journey?

_____
_____
_____
_____

**My Personal Affirmation for Today:**

_____
_____
_____
_____

***Amen Somebody!***

## Day 14: Healing in God's Word

**Affirmation**: I find healing and comfort in the promises of God's word.

*Psalm 107:20 - "He sent out his word and healed them; he rescued them from the grave."*

**Reflective Question**: Which of God's promises bring me the most comfort and healing?

_____
_____
_____
_____

**My Personal Affirmation for Today:**

_____
_____
_____
_____

*Amen Somebody!*

## Day 15: Healing Through God's Grace

**Affirmation**: I am healed and renewed by the grace of God.

*2 Corinthians 12:9 - "My grace is sufficient for you, for my power is made perfect in weakness."*

**Reflective Question**: How can I embrace God's grace in my journey towards healing?

_____

_____

_____

_____

**My Personal Affirmation for Today:**

_____

_____

_____

_____

***Amen Somebody!**

## Day 16: The Peace of Surrender

**Affirmation**: In surrendering my struggles to God, I find peace and healing.

*Matthew 11:28 - "Come to me, all you who are weary and burdened, and I will give you rest."*

**Reflective Question**: What burdens do I need to surrender to God to find peace and healing?

_____
_____
_____
_____

**My Personal Affirmation for Today:**

_____
_____
_____
_____

*Amen Somebody!*

## Day 17: Courage in Healing

**Affirmation**: I have the courage to face my healing journey with God's help.

*Joshua 1:9 - "Have I not commanded you? Be strong and courageous. Do not be afraid; do not be discouraged, for the Lord your God will be with you wherever you go."*

**Reflective Question**: What aspect of my healing journey requires more courage, and how can I find that courage in God?

_____

_____

_____

_____

**My Personal Affirmation for Today:**

_____

_____

_____

_____

***Amen Somebody!***

## Day 18: Healing in Wholeness

**Affirmation**: God's healing touch brings wholeness to my body, mind, and spirit.

*1 Thessalonians 5:23 - "May God himself, the God of peace, sanctify you through and through. May your whole spirit, soul and body be kept blameless at the coming of our Lord Jesus Christ."*

**Reflective Question**: In what ways am I experiencing healing in different areas of my life?

_____

_____

_____

_____


**My Personal Affirmation for Today:**

_____

_____

_____

*Amen Somebody!*

## Day 19: Trusting God's Healing Path

**Affirmation**: I trust the path of healing God has set before me.

*Proverbs 3:5-6 - "Trust in the Lord with all your heart and lean not on your own understanding; in all your ways submit to him, and he will make your paths straight."*

**Reflective Question**: How can I show trust in the healing path God has chosen for me?

_____

_____

_____

_____

**My Personal Affirmation for Today:**

_____

_____

_____

*Amen Somebody!*

## Day 20: Gratitude for Healing Progress

**Affirmation**: I am thankful for every step of progress in my healing journey.

*Psalm 9:1 - "I will give thanks to the Lord with my whole heart; I will recount all of your wonderful deeds."*

**Reflective Question**: What progress in my healing journey can I be thankful for today?

_____
_____
_____
_____

**My Personal Affirmation for Today:**

_____
_____
_____
_____

*Amen Somebody!*

*365 Days Affirmed*

## Day 21: The Strength of God's Love

**Affirmation**: I am strengthened and healed by the power of God's love.

*Romans 8:37-39 - "No, in all these things we are more than conquerors through him who loved us."*

**Reflective Question**: How does the strength of God's love aid in my healing?

_____
_____
_____
_____

**My Personal Affirmation for Today:**

_____
_____
_____
_____

*Amen Somebody!*

## Day 22: Healing in God's Faithfulness

**Affirmation**: I find healing in the faithfulness and steadfast love of God.

*Lamentations 3:22-23 - "The steadfast love of the Lord never ceases; his mercies never come to an end; they are new every morning; great is your faithfulness."*

**Reflective Question**: How have I experienced God's faithfulness and steadfast love in my healing journey?

_____

_____

_____

_____

**My Personal Affirmation for Today:**

_____

_____

_____

_____

*Amen Somebody!*

## Day 23: Overcoming Through God's Power

**Affirmation**: Through God's power, I overcome obstacles in my path to healing.
*Philippians 4:13 - "I can do all things through Christ who strengthens me."*
**Reflective Question**: What obstacles in my healing journey am I overcoming through God's strength?

_____
_____
_____
_____

**My Personal Affirmation for Today:**

_____
_____
_____
_____

*Amen Somebody!*

## Day 24: The Comfort of God's Promise

**Affirmation**: I am comforted by God's promise to be with me in times of need.

*Deuteronomy 31:6 - "Be strong and courageous. Do not be afraid or terrified because of them, for the Lord your God goes with you; he will never leave you nor forsake you."*

**Reflective Question**: How does the promise of God's constant presence bring comfort in my healing?

_____

_____

_____

_____

**My Personal Affirmation for Today:**

_____

_____

_____

*Amen Somebody!*

## Day 25: Healing Through Worship

**Affirmation**: In worship, I connect with God's healing presence.

*Psalm 147:1 - "Praise the Lord. How good it is to sing praises to our God, how pleasant and fitting to praise him!"*

**Reflective Question**: How can worship and praise bring healing into my life?

_____
_____
_____
_____

**My Personal Affirmation for Today:**

_____
_____
_____
_____

*Amen Somebody!*

## Day 26: The Hope of God's Healing

**Affirmation**: I hold onto the hope of complete healing in God's time.

*Romans 15:13 - "May the God of hope fill you with all joy and peace as you trust in him, so that you may overflow with hope by the power of the Holy Spirit."*

**Reflective Question**: How does hope in God's timing influence my healing process?

_____

_____

_____

_____

**My Personal Affirmation for Today:**

_____

_____

_____

_____

*<div align="right">Amen Somebody!</div>*

## Day 27: Reflecting God's Healing Love

**Affirmation**: I reflect God's healing love in my interactions with others.

*1 Peter 4:8 - "Above all, love each other deeply, because love covers over a multitude of sins."*

**Reflective Question**: How can I be a vessel of God's healing love to others?

_____
_____
_____
_____

**My Personal Affirmation for Today:**

_____
_____
_____
_____

*Amen Somebody!*

## Day 28: The Power of God's Word in Healing

**Affirmation**: God's word is a source of healing and strength for me.

*Psalm 107:20 - "He sent out his word and healed them; he rescued them from the grave."*

**Reflective Question**: How has God's word been a source of healing in my life?

_____
_____
_____
_____

**My Personal Affirmation for Today:**

_____
_____
_____

*Amen Somebody!*

## Day 29: Embracing Inner Peace

**Affirmation**: I embrace the inner peace that comes from God's healing touch.

*John 14:27 - "Peace I leave with you; my peace I give you. I do not give to you as the world gives. Do not let your hearts be troubled and do not be afraid."*

**Reflective Question**: How can I cultivate and maintain the inner peace given by God in my healing process?

_____

_____

_____

_____

**My Personal Affirmation for Today:**

_____

_____

_____

_____

*Amen Somebody!*

*Amen Somebody!*

## Day 30: Celebrating Healing Progress

**Affirmation**: I celebrate every step of progress in my journey of healing.

*Isaiah 41:10 - "So do not fear, for I am with you; do not be dismayed, for I am your God. I will strengthen you and help you; I will uphold you with my righteous right hand."*

**Reflective Question**: What milestones in my healing journey can I celebrate today?

_____

_____

_____

_____

**My Personal Affirmation for Today:**

_____

_____

_____

_____

*Amen Somebody!*

## Day 31: Continuous Journey of Healing

**Affirmation**: I acknowledge that healing is a continuous journey, guided by God's hand. *Philippians 1:6 - "Being confident of this, that he who began a good work in you will carry it on to completion until the day of Christ Jesus."*

**Reflective Question**: How can I remain committed to my healing journey, trusting in God's ongoing work in my life?

_____

_____

_____

_____

**My Personal Affirmation for Today:**

_____

_____

_____

_____

***Amen Somebody!***

# November: 30 Days | Forgiveness

*365 Days Affirmed*

## Day 1: Embracing Forgiveness

**Affirmation**: Today, I choose to embrace forgiveness as a path to peace.

*Colossians 3:13 - "Bear with each other and forgive one another if any of you has a grievance against someone. Forgive as the Lord forgave you."*

**Reflective Question**: What steps can I take today to cultivate a forgiving heart?

_____

_____

_____

_____

**My Personal Affirmation for Today:**

_____

_____

_____

_____

### *Amen Somebody!*

*Amen Somebody!*

## Day 2: Letting Go of Resentment

**Affirmation**: I let go of resentment and open my heart to healing through forgiveness.
*Ephesians 4:31-32 - "Get rid of all bitterness, rage and anger, brawling and slander, along with every form of malice. Be kind and compassionate to one another, forgiving each other, just as in Christ God forgave you."*
**Reflective Question**: What resentments am I holding onto that I need to release through forgiveness?

_____

_____

_____

_____

**My Personal Affirmation for Today:**

_____

_____

_____

***Amen Somebody!***

## Day 3: Forgiveness and Love

**Affirmation**: Forgiveness is an act of love, and I choose to love generously.

*1 Peter 4:8 - "Above all, love each other deeply, because love covers over a multitude of sins."*

**Reflective Question**: How can practicing forgiveness be an expression of deep love in my life?

_____

_____

_____

_____

**My Personal Affirmation for Today:**

_____

_____

_____

_____

*Amen Somebody!*

## Day 4: The Freedom of Forgiveness

**Affirmation**: In forgiving others, I find freedom and peace for myself.

*Matthew 6:14-15 - "For if you forgive other people when they sin against you, your heavenly Father will also forgive you. But if you do not forgive others their sins, your Father will not forgive your sins."*

**Reflective Question**: How does forgiving others bring freedom and peace into my life?

_____

_____

_____

_____

**My Personal Affirmation for Today:**

_____

_____

_____

_____

*****Amen Somebody!*****

## Day 5: Healing Through Forgiveness

**Affirmation**: Forgiveness is a pathway to healing and renewal.

*Psalm 147:3 - "He heals the brokenhearted and binds up their wounds."*

**Reflective Question**: In what ways has forgiveness started the healing process in my life?

_____
_____
_____
_____

**My Personal Affirmation for Today:**

_____
_____
_____
_____

***Amen Somebody!***

## Day 6: The Strength to Forgive

**Affirmation**: I have the strength to forgive, guided by God's love and grace.

*Philippians 4:13 - "I can do all this through him who gives me strength."*

**Reflective Question**: How can I draw on God's strength to help me forgive those who have wronged me?

_____

_____

_____

_____

**My Personal Affirmation for Today:**

_____

_____

_____

*Amen Somebody!*

## Day 7: Self-Forgiveness

**Affirmation**: "I extend forgiveness to myself for past mistakes and embrace God's grace."

*Isaiah 43:25 - "I, even I, am he who blots out your transgressions, for my own sake, and remembers your sins no more."*

**Reflective Question**: What do I need to forgive myself for, and how can I embrace God's grace in doing so?

_____

_____

_____

_____

**My Personal Affirmation for Today:**

_____

_____

_____

_____

*Amen Somebody!*

## Day 8: Understanding in Forgiveness

**Affirmation**: I seek to understand others, which aids me in the process of forgiveness.

*Proverbs 19:11 - "A person's wisdom yields patience; it is to one's glory to overlook an offense."*

**Reflective Question**: How can understanding the perspectives of others help me in forgiving them?

_____
_____
_____
_____

**My Personal Affirmation for Today:**

_____
_____
_____
_____

*Amen Somebody!*

## Day 9: Releasing Anger

**Affirmation**: I release anger and bitterness, choosing forgiveness to lighten my heart.

*Ephesians 4:26-27 - "In your anger do not sin: Do not let the sun go down while you are still angry, and do not give the devil a foothold."*

**Reflective Question**: What anger or bitterness can I release today through forgiveness?

_____

_____

_____

_____

**My Personal Affirmation for Today:**

_____

_____

_____

*Amen Somebody!*

## Day 10: The Gift of Mercy

**Affirmation**: I offer mercy through forgiveness, just as I have received mercy.

*Luke 6:36 - "Be merciful, just as your Father is merciful."*

**Reflective Question**: How can showing mercy through forgiveness improve my relationships?

_____

_____

_____

_____

**My Personal Affirmation for Today:**

_____

_____

_____

_____

*Amen Somebody!*

## Day 11: Forgiveness as a Decision

**Affirmation**: I decide to forgive, not based on feelings, but as a choice of will.

*Matthew 18:21-22 - "Then Peter came to Jesus and asked, 'Lord, how many times shall I forgive my brother or sister who sins against me? Up to seven times?' Jesus answered, 'I tell you, not seven times, but seventy-seven times.'"*

**Reflective Question**: What decision can I make today to forgive someone, even if I don't feel like it?

_____

_____


**My Personal Affirmation for Today:**

_____

_____

_____

*Amen Somebody!*

*Amen Somebody!*

## Day 12: The Path to Peace

**Affirmation**: Forgiveness is my path to peace and harmony.

*Romans 12:18 - "If it is possible, as far as it depends on you, live at peace with everyone."*

**Reflective Question**: How does forgiveness lead me towards a life of peace and harmony?

_____

_____

_____

_____

**My Personal Affirmation for Today:**

_____

_____

_____

_____

*Amen Somebody!*

## Day 13: Embracing Compassion

**Affirmation**: I embrace compassion and empathy, which guide me to forgive.

*Colossians 3:12 - "Therefore, as God's chosen people, holy and dearly loved, clothe yourselves with compassion, kindness, humility, gentleness and patience."*

**Reflective Question**: How can developing compassion and empathy aid in my forgiveness of others?

_____

_____

_____

_____

**My Personal Affirmation for Today:**

_____

_____

_____

_____

***Amen Somebody!***

## Day 14: The Joy of Reconciliation

**Affirmation**: I find joy in the reconciliation that comes from true forgiveness.

*2 Corinthians 5:18 - "All this is from God, who reconciled us to himself through Christ and gave us the ministry of reconciliation."*

**Reflective Question**: What joy have I found in past experiences of reconciliation through forgiveness?

_____

_____

_____

_____

**My Personal Affirmation for Today:**

_____

_____

_____

_____

***Amen Somebody!***

## Day 15: Healing Power of Forgiveness

**Affirmation**: I acknowledge the healing power of forgiveness in my life.

*James 5:16 - "Therefore confess your sins to each other and pray for each other so that you may be healed. The prayer of a righteous person is powerful and effective."*

**Reflective Question**: How has forgiveness brought healing into my life and relationships?

_____

_____

_____

_____

**My Personal Affirmation for Today:**

_____

_____

_____

_____

*Amen Somebody!*

## Day 16: Letting Go of the Past

**Affirmation**: I choose to let go of the past and forgive those who have hurt me.

*Isaiah 43:18-19 - "Forget the former things; do not dwell on the past. See, I am doing a new thing! Now it springs up; do you not perceive it?"*

**Reflective Question**: What past hurts do I need to release through forgiveness to move forward?

_____

_____

_____

_____

**My Personal Affirmation for Today:**

_____

_____

_____

*Amen Somebody!*

## Day 17: Forgiveness and Inner Peace

**Affirmation**: Forgiveness brings me closer to achieving inner peace.

*Matthew 5:9 - "Blessed are the peacemakers, for they will be called children of God."*

**Reflective Question**: How does practicing forgiveness contribute to my inner peace?

_____

_____

_____

_____

**My Personal Affirmation for Today:**

_____

_____

_____

_____

*Amen Somebody!*

## Day 18: The Freedom in Forgiving Ourselves

**Affirmation**: I find freedom in forgiving myself for my own mistakes.

*Psalm 32:5 - "Then I acknowledged my sin to you and did not cover up my iniquity. I said, 'I will confess my transgressions to the Lord.' And you forgave the guilt of my sin."*

**Reflective Question**: What do I need to forgive myself for, and how can this forgiveness free me?

_____

_____

_____

_____

**My Personal Affirmation for Today:**

_____

_____

_____

*Amen Somebody!*

## Day 19: The Blessing of Second Chances

**Affirmation**: I am thankful for the second chances that forgiveness offers.

*Lamentations 3:22-23 - "Because of the Lord's great love we are not consumed, for his compassions never fail. They are new every morning; great is your faithfulness."*

**Reflective Question**: How have I benefited from the second chances that come with forgiveness?

_____

_____

_____

_____

**My Personal Affirmation for Today:**

_____

_____

_____

_____

*Amen Somebody!*

*Amen Somebody!*

## Day 20: Cultivating a Forgiving Heart

**Affirmation**: Each day, I cultivate a forgiving heart, reflecting God's love.

*Ephesians 4:2 - "Be completely humble and gentle; be patient, bearing with one another in love."*

**Reflective Question**: What daily practices can help me cultivate a more forgiving heart?

_____
_____
_____
_____

**My Personal Affirmation for Today:**

_____
_____
_____
_____

*Amen Somebody!*

## Day 21: The Power of Releasing Grudges

**Affirmation**: I release grudges and embrace the freedom that comes with forgiveness.

*Hebrews 12:15 - "See to it that no one falls short of the grace of God and that no bitter root grows up to cause trouble and defile many."*

**Reflective Question**: What grudges am I holding onto that I need to release for my well-being?

_____

_____

_____

_____

**My Personal Affirmation for Today:**

_____

_____

_____

_____

*Amen Somebody!*

## Day 22: Embrace Unconditional Forgiveness

**Affirmation**: I strive to offer forgiveness unconditionally, reflecting God's unconditional love.

*Matthew 18:21-22 - "Then Peter came to him and asked, 'Lord, how often should I forgive someone who sins against me? Seven times?' 'No, not seven times,' Jesus replied, 'but seventy times seven.'"*

**Reflective Question**: How can I practice offering forgiveness unconditionally in my daily life?

_____

_____

_____

**My Personal Affirmation for Today:**

_____

_____

_____

*Amen Somebody!*

*365 Days Affirmed*

## Day 23: The Clarity of Forgiveness

**Affirmation**: Forgiveness brings clarity and understanding to my heart and mind.

*1 Corinthians 13:12 - "Now we see things imperfectly, like puzzling reflections in a mirror, but then we will see everything with perfect clarity."*

**Reflective Question**: In what ways has forgiveness brought clarity and understanding to my life?

_____

_____

_____

_____

**My Personal Affirmation for Today:**

_____

_____

_____

_____

*Amen Somebody!*

*Amen Somebody!*

## Day 24: Growth Through Forgiveness

**Affirmation**: I grow spiritually and emotionally each time I choose to forgive.

*2 Peter 3:18 - "But grow in the grace and knowledge of our Lord and Savior Jesus Christ. To him be glory both now and forever! Amen."*

**Reflective Question**: How has my ability to forgive contributed to my personal growth?

_____
_____
_____
_____

**My Personal Affirmation for Today:**

_____
_____
_____

*Amen Somebody!*

## Day 25: The Lightness of Forgiving

**Affirmation**: Forgiving others lightens my heart and frees my spirit.

*Matthew 11:30 - "For my yoke is easy and my burden is light."*

**Reflective Question**: How has forgiving others lightened the burdens I carry?

_____
_____
_____
_____

**My Personal Affirmation for Today:**

_____
_____
_____
_____

***Amen Somebody!***

## Day 26: Harmony Through Forgiveness

**Affirmation**: I foster harmony and understanding through the act of forgiveness. *Romans 12:16 - "Live in harmony with one another. Do not be proud, but be willing to associate with people of low position. Do not be conceited."*
**Reflective Question**: How does forgiveness help me live in harmony with others?

_____

_____

_____

_____

**My Personal Affirmation for Today:**

_____

_____

_____

_____

*Amen Somebody!*

## Day 27: The Gift of Forgiveness

**Affirmation**: I view forgiveness as a precious gift that I can give and receive.

*Ephesians 1:7 - "In him we have redemption through his blood, the forgiveness of sins, in accordance with the riches of God's grace."*

**Reflective Question**: How do I perceive forgiveness as a gift in my life?

_____

_____

_____

_____

**My Personal Affirmation for Today:**

_____

_____

_____

_____

*Amen Somebody!*

## Day 28: The Wisdom in Forgiveness

**Affirmation**: I gain wisdom and insight each time I choose to forgive.

*James 3:17 - "But the wisdom that comes from heaven is first of all pure; then peace-loving, considerate, submissive, full of mercy and good fruit, impartial and sincere."*

**Reflective Question**: What wisdom have I gained through experiences of forgiveness?

_____

_____

_____

_____

**My Personal Affirmation for Today:**

_____

_____

_____

_____

*Amen Somebody!*

## Day 29: The Serenity of Forgiveness

**Affirmation**: I find serenity and calmness in the act of forgiving.

*Philippians 4:7 - "And the peace of God, which transcends all understanding, will guard your hearts and your minds in Christ Jesus."*

**Reflective Question**: How does the act of forgiving bring peace and serenity into my life?

_____
_____
_____
_____

**My Personal Affirmation for Today:**

_____
_____
_____
_____

*Amen Somebody!*

## Day 30: Continuous Forgiveness

**Affirmation**: I recognize forgiveness as a continuous journey, essential for my spiritual growth.

*Colossians 1:10 - "So that you may live a life worthy of the Lord and please him in every way: bearing fruit in every good work, growing in the knowledge of God."*

**Reflective Question**: How will I continue to incorporate forgiveness into my daily life for ongoing spiritual growth?

_____

_____

_____

**My Personal Affirmation for Today:**

_____

_____

_____

_____

*Amen Somebody!*

# December: 31 Days | New Beginnings

*Amen Somebody!*

## Day 1: Embracing New Beginnings

**Affirmation**: Today, I open my heart to the new beginnings that await me.

*Isaiah 43:19 - "See, I am doing a new thing! Now it springs up; do you not perceive it? I am making a way in the wilderness and streams in the wasteland."*

**Reflective Question**: What new beginning am I being called to embrace today?

_____

_____

_____

_____

**My Personal Affirmation for Today:**

_____

_____

_____

*Amen Somebody!*

## Day 2: Letting Go of the Old

**Affirmation**: I let go of the old to make room for new blessings and opportunities.

*Ephesians 4:22-24 - "You were taught, with regard to your former way of life, to put off your old self, which is being corrupted by its deceitful desires; to be made new in the attitude of your minds; and to put on the new self, created to be like God in true righteousness and holiness."*

**Reflective Question**: What old habits or thoughts do I need to let go of to welcome new beginnings?

_____

_____

_____

**My Personal Affirmation for Today:**

_____

_____

_____

*Amen Somebody!*

*Amen Somebody!*

## Day 3: Courage for New Adventures

**Affirmation**: I have the courage to step into new adventures and experiences.

*Joshua 1:9 - "Have I not commanded you? Be strong and courageous. Do not be afraid; do not be discouraged, for the Lord your God will be with you wherever you go."*

**Reflective Question**: What new adventure requires my courage today?

_____
_____
_____
_____

**My Personal Affirmation for Today:**

_____
_____
_____
_____

*Amen Somebody!*

## Day 4: New Opportunities for Growth

**Affirmation**: Every new day is an opportunity for growth and renewal.

*Lamentations 3:22-23 - "Because of the Lord's great love we are not consumed, for his compassions never fail. They are new every morning; great is your faithfulness."*

**Reflective Question**: How can I use today's opportunities to grow and renew myself?

_____

_____

_____

_____

**My Personal Affirmation for Today:**

_____

_____

_____

_____

*Amen Somebody!*

## Day 5: Trusting in New Paths

**Affirmation**: I trust in the new paths that God is leading me on.

*Proverbs 3:5-6 - "Trust in the Lord with all your heart and lean not on your own understanding; in all your ways submit to him, and he will make your paths straight."*

**Reflective Question**: How can I show trust in the new paths I am exploring today?

_____

_____

_____

_____

**My Personal Affirmation for Today:**

_____

_____

_____

_____

### *Amen Somebody!*

*365 Days Affirmed*

## Day 6: New Beginnings in Relationships

**Affirmation**: I welcome new beginnings in my relationships, fostering love and understanding. *Romans 12:10 - "Be devoted to one another in love. Honor one another above yourselves."*

**Reflective Question**: What new beginnings can I foster in my relationships today?

_____
_____
_____
_____

**My Personal Affirmation for Today:**

_____
_____
_____
_____

*Amen Somebody!*

*Amen Somebody!*

## Day 7: The Joy of New Discoveries

**Affirmation**: I embrace the joy and excitement of new discoveries in my life.

*Psalm 16:11 - "You make known to me the path of life; in your presence there is fullness of joy; at your right hand are pleasures forevermore."*

**Reflective Question**: What new discoveries am I excited about today?

_____

_____

_____

_____

**My Personal Affirmation for Today:**

_____

_____

_____

_____

*Amen Somebody!*

*365 Days Affirmed*

## Day 8: Renewed Mindset

**Affirmation**: I cultivate a renewed mindset, open to positive changes and new ideas.

*Romans 12:2 - "Do not conform to the pattern of this world, but be transformed by the renewing of your mind. Then you will be able to test and approve what God's will is—his good, pleasing and perfect will."*

**Reflective Question**: How can I renew my mindset today to be more open to new ideas and changes?

_____
_____
_____

**My Personal Affirmation for Today:**

_____
_____
_____
_____

*Amen Somebody!*

## Day 9: Overcoming Fear of the New

**Affirmation**: I overcome any fears of the unknown and embrace new beginnings with confidence.

*2 Timothy 1:7 - "For God has not given us a spirit of fear, but of power and of love and of a sound mind."*

**Reflective Question**: What fears do I need to overcome to embrace new beginnings confidently?

_____
_____
_____
_____

**My Personal Affirmation for Today:**

_____
_____
_____
_____

*Amen Somebody!*

*365 Days Affirmed*

## Day 10: New Strength Each Day

**Affirmation**: Each new day brings me strength and hope for the journey ahead.

*Isaiah 40:31 - "But those who hope in the Lord will renew their strength. They will soar on wings like eagles; they will run and not grow weary, they will walk and not be faint."*

**Reflective Question**: How does each new day strengthen my hope and resolve?

_____

_____

_____

_____

**My Personal Affirmation for Today:**

_____

_____

_____

_____

*Amen Somebody!*

*Amen Somebody!*

## Day 11: Embracing Change

**Affirmation**: I embrace change as a natural and beneficial part of life.

*Ecclesiastes 3:1 - "To everything there is a season, and a time to every purpose under the heaven."*

**Reflective Question**: What changes am I currently embracing, and how are they beneficial to my life?

_____

_____

_____

_____

**My Personal Affirmation for Today:**

_____

_____

_____

_____

*Amen Somebody!*

## Day 12: New Perspectives

**Affirmation**: I seek and embrace new perspectives that enrich my understanding. *Proverbs 2:6 - "For the Lord gives wisdom; from his mouth come knowledge and understanding."*

**Reflective Question**: What new perspectives can I seek today to enrich my understanding?

_____
_____
_____
_____

**My Personal Affirmation for Today:**

_____
_____
_____
_____

***Amen Somebody!***

## Day 13: Fresh Starts

**Affirmation**: I value each day as a fresh start and a new opportunity to grow.

*Psalm 118:24 - "This is the day that the Lord has made; let us rejoice and be glad in it."*

**Reflective Question**: How can I make the most of this fresh start today?

_____
_____
_____
_____

**My Personal Affirmation for Today:**

_____
_____
_____
_____

*Amen Somebody!*

## Day 14: New Beginnings in Faith

**Affirmation**: My faith is renewed each day, opening doors to new beginnings.

*Hebrews 11:1 - "Now faith is confidence in what we hope for and assurance about what we do not see."*

**Reflective Question**: How does my faith lead me to new beginnings and opportunities?

_____
_____
_____
_____

**My Personal Affirmation for Today:**

_____
_____
_____
_____

*Amen Somebody!*

*Amen Somebody!*

## Day 15: Gratitude for New Opportunities

**Affirmation**: I am grateful for every new opportunity that comes my way.

*James 1:17 - "Every good and perfect gift is from above, coming down from the Father of the heavenly lights, who does not change like shifting shadows."*

**Reflective Question**: What new opportunities am I grateful for today?

_____

_____

_____

_____

**My Personal Affirmation for Today:**

_____

_____

_____

_____

*Amen Somebody!*

*365 Days Affirmed*

## Day 16: New Beginnings in Love

**Affirmation**: I open my heart to new beginnings in love and relationships.

*1 Corinthians 13:4-7 - "Love is patient, love is kind. It does not envy, it does not boast, it is not proud. It does not dishonor others, it is not self-seeking, it is not easily angered, it keeps no record of wrongs."*

**Reflective Question**: How can I foster new beginnings in my relationships through love?

_____

_____

_____

_____

**My Personal Affirmation for Today:**

_____

_____

_____

_____

*Amen Somebody!*

*Amen Somebody!*

## Day 17: The Adventure of New Experiences

**Affirmation**: I embrace the adventure and learning that come with new experiences.

*Psalm 34:8 - "Taste and see that the Lord is good; blessed is the one who takes refuge in him."*

**Reflective Question**: What new experiences am I looking forward to, and what can I learn from them?

_____

_____

_____

_____

**My Personal Affirmation for Today:**

_____

_____

_____

_____

*Amen Somebody!*

## Day 18: New Beginnings in Work and Career

**Affirmation**: I am open to new paths and opportunities in my work and career.

*Proverbs 16:3 - "Commit to the Lord whatever you do, and he will establish your plans."*

**Reflective Question**: What new paths or opportunities in my career am I exploring or hoping for?

_____

_____

_____

_____

**My Personal Affirmation for Today:**

_____

_____

_____

_____

*Amen Somebody!*

## Day 19: Spiritual Renewal

**Affirmation**: I seek and embrace spiritual renewal as a vital part of my life.

*2 Corinthians 4:16 - "Therefore we do not lose heart. Though outwardly we are wasting away, yet inwardly we are being renewed day by day."*

**Reflective Question**: In what ways am I experiencing spiritual renewal, and how is it impacting my life?

_____

_____

_____

_____

**My Personal Affirmation for Today:**

_____

_____

_____

*Amen Somebody!*

## Day 20: Healthy New Beginnings

**Affirmation**: I commit to new beginnings in health and wellness, honoring my body and mind.

*1 Corinthians 6:19-20 - "Do you not know that your bodies are temples of the Holy Spirit, who is in you, whom you have received from God? You are not your own; you were bought at a price. Therefore honor God with your bodies."*

**Reflective Question**: What new commitments can I make for my health and wellness?

_____

_____

_____

**My Personal Affirmation for Today:**

_____

_____

_____

### *Amen Somebody!*

*Amen Somebody!*

## Day 21: Learning from New Challenges

**Affirmation**: I view new challenges as opportunities to learn and grow.

*James 1:2-4 - "Consider it pure joy, my brothers and sisters, whenever you face trials of many kinds, because you know that the testing of your faith produces perseverance."*

**Reflective Question**: What recent challenges have I faced, and what have I learned from them?

_____

_____

_____

_____

**My Personal Affirmation for Today:**

_____

_____

_____

*Amen Somebody!*

## Day 22: Embracing Change with Positivity

**Affirmation**: I embrace change positively, trusting that it leads to personal growth.

*Romans 8:28 - "And we know that in all things God works for the good of those who love him, who have been called according to his purpose."*

**Reflective Question**: How can I approach changes in my life with a positive and trusting attitude?

_____
_____
_____
_____

**My Personal Affirmation for Today:**

_____
_____
_____
_____

*Amen Somebody!*

*Amen Somebody!*

## Day 23: New Perspectives on Challenges

**Affirmation**: I seek new perspectives in facing challenges, turning obstacles into opportunities. *Philippians 4:13 - "I can do all this through him who gives me strength."*

**Reflective Question**: How can I view my current challenges as opportunities for growth and learning?

_____

_____

_____

_____

**My Personal Affirmation for Today:**

_____

_____

_____

_____

*Amen Somebody!*

## Day 24: Fresh Beginnings Each Morning

**Affirmation**: Each morning, I welcome fresh beginnings and new mercies.

*Lamentations 3:22-23 - "The steadfast love of the Lord never ceases; his mercies never come to an end; they are new every morning; great is your faithfulness."*

**Reflective Question**: What new mercies and beginnings am I thankful for this morning?

_____
_____
_____
_____

**My Personal Affirmation for Today:**

_____
_____
_____
_____

*Amen Somebody!*

## Day 25: New Beginnings in Creativity

**Affirmation**: I explore new beginnings in creativity, expressing myself freely.

*Exodus 35:31-32 - "and he has filled him with the Spirit of God, with wisdom, with understanding, with knowledge and with all kinds of skills—to make artistic designs for work in gold, silver and bronze."*

**Reflective Question**: How can I embrace new beginnings in my creative endeavors today?

_____

_____

_____

_____

**My Personal Affirmation for Today:**

_____

_____

_____

_____

*Amen Somebody!*

## Day 26: Growth in New Environments

**Affirmation**: I am open to growth and learning in new environments and situations.

*Jeremiah 17:7-8 - "But blessed is the one who trusts in the Lord, whose confidence is in him. They will be like a tree planted by the water that sends out its roots by the stream."*

**Reflective Question**: How can I embrace and grow in the new environments I find myself in?

_____
_____
_____
_____

**My Personal Affirmation for Today:**

_____
_____
_____
_____

*Amen Somebody!*

## Day 27: New Beginnings in Faith

**Affirmation**: I embrace new beginnings in my faith journey, trusting in God's guidance.

*Proverbs 3:5-6 - "Trust in the Lord with all your heart and lean not on your own understanding; in all your ways submit to him, and he will make your paths straight."*

**Reflective Question**: How am I experiencing new beginnings in my faith journey?

_____

_____

_____

_____

**My Personal Affirmation for Today:**

_____

_____

_____

*Amen Somebody!*

## Day 28: Renewed Hope

**Affirmation**: I hold onto renewed hope as I embark on new journeys.

*Romans 15:13 - "May the God of hope fill you with all joy and peace as you trust in him, so that you may overflow with hope by the power of the Holy Spirit."*

**Reflective Question**: What new hopes am I holding onto today?

_____

_____

_____

_____

**My Personal Affirmation for Today:**

_____

_____

_____

_____

**Amen Somebody!**

*Amen Somebody!*

## Day 29: New Beginnings in my Community

**Affirmation**: I value and seek new beginnings in my community, building meaningful connections.

*Hebrews 10:24-25 - "And let us consider how we may spur one another on toward love and good deeds, not giving up meeting together, as some are in the habit of doing, but encouraging one another—and all the more as you see the Day approaching."*

**Reflective Question**: How can I foster stronger new beginnings in my community?

_____

_____

_____

**My Personal Affirmation for Today:**

_____

_____

_____

*Amen Somebody!*

*365 Days Affirmed*

## Day 30: The Power of New Intentions

**Affirmation**: I set powerful new intentions, aligning them with my values and goals.

*Habakkuk 2:2-3 - "Then the Lord replied: 'Write down the revelation and make it plain on tablets so that a herald may run with it. For the revelation awaits an appointed time; it speaks of the end and will not prove false. Though it lingers, wait for it; it will certainly come and will not delay.'"*

**Reflective Question**: What new intentions can I set today to align with my values and goals?

_____

_____

_____

**My Personal Affirmation for Today:**

_____

_____

_____

***Amen Somebody!***

*Amen Somebody!*

## Day 31: Celebrating Growth and New Beginnings

**Affirmation**: I celebrate the growth and progress I have made in embracing new beginnings.

*Psalm 126:3 - "The Lord has done great things for us, and we are filled with joy."*

**Reflective Question**: How can I celebrate the growth and new beginnings I have experienced this month?

_____
_____
_____
_____

**My Personal Affirmation for Today:**

_____
_____
_____

*Amen Somebody!*

*365 Days Affirmed*

*Amen Somebody!*

## Afterword…

As we reach the conclusion of *365 Days Affirmed*, it's important to reflect on the journey we've undertaken together. This book was not just a collection of affirmations; it was an invitation to a daily practice of reflection, spiritual growth, and personal transformation.

Throughout the year, you've been guided through various themes — from embracing healing and forgiveness to welcoming new beginnings. Each day offered a unique affirmation, grounded in Scripture, to help you focus your thoughts and align your spirit with God's Word. The reflective questions were designed to encourage deeper introspection, helping you to apply these truths to your own life.

In this journey, you've likely encountered days where the affirmations spoke directly to your heart, addressing the very challenges or aspirations you were facing. There may have been other days where the words didn't resonate as strongly, yet they still planted seeds of wisdom and faith in your soul.

As you continue your spiritual walk, remember that the practice of affirmation is a powerful tool. It's a way to renew your mind daily, as Romans 12:2 reminds us, not conforming to the pattern of this world but being transformed by the renewing of your mind. This transformation is ongoing — a journey rather than a destination.

May you carry the lessons and insights from this book into each new day. Let the affirmations be a source of strength, comfort, and guidance as you navigate the complexities of life. Remember, God's word is a lamp unto your feet and a light

*Amen Somebody!*

unto your path (Psalm 119:105). It's my prayer that these affirmations, rooted in His Word, continue to light your way.

Thank you for allowing this book to be a part of your spiritual journey. May God's peace, love, and wisdom be with you always. Amen Somebody!

Theresa Y. Brown

Theresa Y. Brown can be contacted via email at theresa@theresaybrown.com or via her website www.theresaybrown.com.

*Amen Somebody!*

## Scriptural References / Holy Bible

| | |
|---|---|
| Philippians 4:13 | Hebrews 12:1 |
| Joshua 1:9 | Psalm 46:10 |
| James 1:12 | Exodus 35:31-32 |
| Proverbs 3:26 | Psalm 150:6 |
| Isaiah 41:10 | Jeremiah 29:11 |
| Mark 9:23 | Ephesians 5:15-16 |
| Psalm 46:1-2 | 1 Peter 4:10 |
| John 14:27 | Psalm 37:4 |
| Romans 15:13 | Isaiah 43:19 |
| 1 Thessalonians 5:18 | James 1:5 |
| 2 Timothy 1:7 | Matthew 5:16 |
| James 1:5 | Romans 5:3-4 |
| Ephesians 4:15 | Psalm 46:10 |
| 1 Corinthians 16:14 | 2 Peter 3:18 |
| Jeremiah 29:11 | Galatians 5:13 |
| Nehemiah 8:10 | 2 Timothy 1:7 |
| Matthew 5:5 | 1 Thessalonians 5:18 |
| Romans 12:18 | 1 Samuel 16:7 |
| 1 Samuel 16:7 | Philippians 2:13 |
| Colossians 3:12 | Habakkuk 2:2 |
| 1 Corinthians 9:24 | Joshua 1:9 |
| Hebrews 10:24 | Ecclesiastes 3:1 |
| Psalm 46:10 | Psalm 37:7 |
| Proverbs 11:25 | Romans 8:28 |
| Galatians 6:9 | Psalm 139:14 |
| Proverbs 10:9 | Philippians 4:8 |
| Exodus 35:31-32 | Proverbs 16:3 |

| | |
|---|---|
| James 4:6 | John 14:27 |
| Ephesians 4:32 | 2 Corinthians 5:17 |
| Psalm 150:6 | Romans 12:12 |
| Galatians 6:9 | Psalm 119:105 |
| Proverbs 3:5-6 | Proverbs 3:6 |
| Isaiah 40:31 | 2 Corinthians 12:9 |
| Psalm 32:8 | Psalm 118:24 |
| Hebrews 11:1 | Philippians 3:13 |
| John 14:27 | Corinthians 13:4 |
| James 2:17 | 1 John 4:19 |
| 1 Thessalonians 5:18 | 1 Peter 4:8 |
| Romans 15:13 | Ephesians 4:2 |
| 1 Corinthians 13:13 | Proverbs 10:12 |
| Philippians 4:13 | 1 Corinthians 16:14 |
| 2 Peter 3:18 | Psalm 107:1 |
| Ephesians 4:32 | Galatians 5:22 |
| Romans 5:3-4 | John 13:34 |
| Hebrews 10:24-25 | Colossians 3:14 |
| Psalm 46:1 | Psalm 147:3 |
| James 1:5 | Hebrews 13:2 |
| Galatians 6:9 | Ephesians 3:18 |
| Jeremiah 17:14 | 2 Peter 3:18 |
| Psalm 28:7 | Matthew 7:12 |
| Proverbs 19:21 | Ecclesiastes 4:9 |
| Jeremiah 29:11 | Luke 6:38 |
| 2 Corinthians 9:7 | Romans 12:2 |
| James 4:6 | Psalm 119:105 |
| Proverbs 11:3 | |
| Colossians 3:12 | |

*365 Days Affirmed*

Made in the USA
Columbia, SC
29 September 2024